# THE L ST PASSENGER TR IN

**Other Books by Robert M. Goldstein**

*The Gentleman from Finland—Adventures
on the Trans-Siberian Express*

*Riding with Reindeer—A Bicycle Odyssey
through Finland, Lapland, and Arctic Norway*

# THE LAST PASSENGER TRAIN

## A Rail Journey across Canada

by

### ROBERT M. GOLDSTEIN

Published by Rivendell Publishing Northwest
Seattle, Washington

Rivendell Publishing Northwest, Seattle, Washington
Copyright © 2020 by Robert M. Goldstein
All rights reserved under International
and Pan American Copyright Conventions.

Published in the United States of America by
Rivendell Publishing Northwest, Seattle, Washington.

This book is a work of nonfiction.

Printed in the United States of America
Library of Congress Catalog Number 2020901420
ISBN (print edition) 978-0-9763288-5-8

*Copyedit by Christopher Chien*
*Book and cover design by Liz Kingslien*
*Cover photo and images: iStock.com*
*About the Author photo property of Robert M. Goldstein*

First Edition, First Printing

**Rivendell Publishing Northwest**
7725 First Avenue NE
Seattle, WA 98115-4003

# TABLE OF CONTENTS

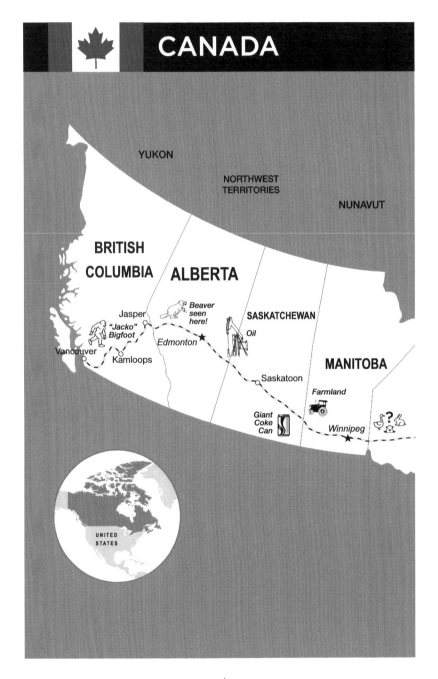

**The Last Passenger Train Route**

Hudson Bay

NEWFOUNDLAND AND LABRADOR

ONTARIO

QUEBEC

Gulf of St. Lawrence

Moose sighting!

Woods and swamp

Québec

NEW BRUNSWICK

Sudbury

Montréal

Bay of Fundy

Halifax

NOVA SCOTIA

Toronto

NORTH ATLANTIC OCEAN

*Dedicated to my dear mother,*
*Magdalena (Maggie)*

# CHAPTER 1

### The Great Hall

UNION STATION is an imposing Beaux-Arts–style limestone and marble building that occupies a city block of prime Toronto real estate. Completed in 1927 during the halcyon days of passenger rail service, the structure's expansive Great Hall—the largest room in Canada—stretches nearly the length of a football field, while the vaulted ceiling reaches 88 feet at its peak. Diffused sunlight percolates from the clerestory windows that line the upper walls and adds to the shrine-like atmosphere. One can easily imagine a bustling scene of men in smart gray suits and fedoras, ladies in long dresses, some in furs, heels clicking on the herringbone-patterned marble floor, while newsboys hawk headlines.

The front doors to this temple dedicated to rail travel are guarded by 22 Roman Tuscan limestone pillars, each weighing 75 tons. Above these columns, chiseled to the side of "Union Station," is inscribed "Grand Trunk Railroad," a term borrowed from the ancient Grand Trunk Road built in the third century BC to link India with Afghanistan. It's obvious why the name was adopted by the Grand Trunk Railroad company, later to become *Canadian National* or CN. From here, all railroad journeys of significance began or ended, including the one thin line that ventured west across the swampy forests of upper Ontario, spanned the great prairie, and then struggled over the Rocky Mountains to the Pacific Ocean. The rival *Canadian Pacific Railroad,* or CPR, could argue that it too once lorded over an equally impressive passenger railroad empire, but its last transcontinental train made its final journey in 1990.

Now there is only one transcontinental train left. Twice a week, under the cover of darkness, *The Canadian* ventures forth from Union Station's vast underground catacomb to make the grand journey west—one of the longest train trips in the world, and the last of the great passenger railroad journeys across Canada.

Ninety years after Prince Edward—Prince of Wales and the future Edward VIII—opened Union Station, wielding a pair of golden scissors to cut the ribbon, Mindy and I find we cannot pass through the great columns. The station is enclosed in cyclone fencing to protect the public from potential construction hazards of ongoing restoration intended to keep this architectural treasure from suffering the fate of other grand stations. We are routed around to the side and enter the station through an improvised side entrance lined with plywood and coated with construction dust.

On this lovely spring day in May 2017, we have come

to ride the transcontinental train. Like most train people, we are early. *The Canadian* does not leave until 10:00 p.m., a lonely hour for this station. While commuters and regional rail traffic make it a busy place during the day, as evening descends after rush hour the station seems almost reluctant to be open for this final send-off. It seems as if the departure of this last train across the continent is an embarrassment to this bustling, hip city. Sending these lumbering 1950s-era silver rail carriages, remnants of a bygone era, off under the cover of darkness seems the only respectable thing to do in these modern times.

One could hardly blame us for our eagerness to board, to at least stake a claim aboard this piece of rolling history before it is too late. Given the reduction of passenger rail service throughout North America, one never knows when the government will pull the final budget plug. We hope never, but then again, long-haul passenger trains are like a species of animal that was once abundant but is now threatened with extinction. Without government subsidies, they will die.[1]

At 9:00 p.m., the Great Hall is nearly deserted, seemingly occupied only by our echoing footsteps and the thrum of roller bags from a handful of potential passengers in the vast chamber, now dimly lit and looking more like a mausoleum than a train station. We make our way

---

1   When we took this trip, *The Canadian* operated two trips a week in the winter and three in the summer. By the time this book was published, the summer trips had been reduced to two.

down a corridor and find baggage check-in. Earlier in the day, we had stored our bags here for later pickup, an amenity provided to first-class passengers. We didn't want them stowed in the baggage car. On a four-day, four-night journey, we will need the stuff in our suitcases.

We wander back into the Great Hall and see, at one end, the entrance to the lounge provided to first-class customers. Here, we find a few fellow passengers lounging on the couches and in the comfortable chairs scattered about the room. Tucked in a corner is a commercial-sized cooler stocked with soft drinks and bottled water. Our train crew circulates, explaining boarding procedures and taking meal reservations for the next day. We nestle into a couch and wait for the boarding call.

The dining car steward stops by and takes our lunch and dinner reservations for the next day. A young woman, bubbling with enthusiasm, introduces herself as Claire, the train's activity coordinator. I didn't know there would be activities to coordinate, but alas, they will be in our future. Wine tasting, movies, lectures in the dome car all await us, according to the effervescent Claire. After she bounds away, I can see that my wife has not fully jumped onto the bandwagon. "That chick needs to calm down," says Mindy, whose only goal now is to get on the train and go to sleep.

Calm returns as the crew moves on to another part of the lounge.

"This is a pleasant way to wait for the train," I say.

Mindy nods in agreement. We are now in place ready to complete a circuitous round trip, both by rail and in life, that began eight years ago.

# CHAPTER 2

### Beginnings

IN 2009, ON A LARK, I bought a pair of first-class tickets for the four-day train trip across Canada. The trip began in Vancouver and ended in Toronto. I say "on a lark" because normally the trip is expensive—at least for a first-class cabin, the only sane way to undertake this journey. Until that time, I was not prone to traveling first class. I was a coach guy all the way, my life a testimony to practical travel frugality. But in the depths of a recession, with the Canadian Dollar languishing against its U.S. counterpart and the grip of an icy winter scaring off customers, the authorities who manage VIA Rail, Canada's answer to Amtrak, decided to deeply discount tickets with the hope of filling its premier train before the more lucrative summer season arrived. Given this opportunity, I pounced and recruited my friend (later to be my wife—more on this to come) Mindy to travel across Canada on the train.

"It will be fun," I said.

"Okay," she said. "But will it be cold?"

"It will be in March. How cold can it possibly get?" I replied.

Apparently, Canada can get very cold in March. I remember clambering off the train at a forlorn station stop called Melville, Saskatchewan. It was 20 degrees below zero (Fahrenheit). Ice caked the wheels of the train. Icicles hung from the carriage like crystal stalactites. Our breath formed clouds that turned to tiny ice crystals, then drifted to the ground. It was beautiful.

The route snaked through the snow-covered Rocky Mountains, then rattled through the rolling hills and flats of the prairie provinces before arching over Lake Superior in upper Ontario through a land of frozen bogs and withered trees. Amid this near-Arctic isolation, we basked in the warmth of our cabin and feasted like royalty. The dining car, featuring new items on the menu every day, was like a fine restaurant on wheels. After partaking of Amtrak fare for most of our train lives, the culinary portion of this trip was an unexpected delight. There was only one problem: As the train made its way east, we breached a time zone every day. This cost us an hour, which meant the intervals between feasts grew shorter the farther east we went. By the time we reached Ontario, we were hardly able to eat because we had so little time in which to digest our previous meal.

Perhaps the most startling aspect of the journey, however, was the end. The conductor, with more than a hint of celebration in his voice, announced that Train Number Two (the one we were aboard) would not only arrive on schedule, but would be an hour early. An hour early! Are you kidding? What planet are we on?

The crew was giddy. Apparently, this was a rare accomplishment. At breakfast, our server explained that the train was perpetually late, sometimes by many hours, because of the need to lay over on sidings to let frequent freight trains pass along the single-track main line. Freight had priority. But in the depths of recession, freight trains were scarce. The single track was clear most of the time. At 8:35 a.m., 65 minutes ahead of schedule, Train Number Two slid into its assigned platform at Toronto's Union Station. Because of the unexpected early arrival, the conductor announced passengers could take extra time packing up and debarking. Finish breakfast if you need to, no need to scamper off the train because the crew was still on duty. We enjoyed the journey so much we had hoped Train Number Two would continue the tradition of tardiness by as many hours as possible so we could experience this excellent trip a little longer. We finally debarked and caught a cab to our hotel, where we waited in the lobby for several hours for our room to be ready. Who knew the train would be an hour early?

The Trans-Canada train trip was now off my bucket list. A good thing, too, because the recession soon ended. Oil became big news in Canada. The economy boomed. The loonie (Canada's dollar, so named because Canada's one-dollar coin features a picture of a loon) soared above the U.S. dollar for the first time in memory. Freight trains returned with a vengeance. As affordable as the trip was in

2009, it now became too costly. Other unexplored travel destinations beckoned. Another train trip across Canada was not a priority.

Mindy and I went to Peru, then Costa Rica. She accompanied me to New York City, where I attended a publisher's conference. The best part of that trip was the journey home, aboard the *Lake Shore Limited* from New York City north along the Hudson River before turning west to Chicago. We next boarded the *Empire Builder* for the three-day trip back to our homes in Seattle. All were first-class. The upgrade, first experienced on *The Canadian*, had become a habit.

Perhaps the biggest journey was the one to the altar, which we took together in August 2015. Careful readers of my last book, *Riding with Reindeer—A Bicycle Odyssey through Finland, Lapland, and Arctic Norway,* may recall a reference to Mindy, who was generous enough to house-sit for me while I pedaled my way through a rainy summer in Finland. We had known each other since 1977, when we shared a house, along with a third roommate, in Walla Walla, Washington. I was a summer intern at the city's daily newspaper. Mindy was beginning her career with the federal government, as a civilian human resource specialist with the U.S. Army. In the ensuing years our lives would take many twists and turns. Her career tour of duty eventually took her to Portland (Oregon), San Francisco (California), Heidelberg and Hanau (Germany), back to San Francisco, then to Sparta (Wisconsin). I ended up in

Seattle. We kept in touch after that summer and sometimes visited. We would both be in other romantic relationships, but our friendship endured over the decades. The other romances did not.

Mindy retired from her career in 2006. She moved to Seattle. Our friendship became even friendlier. We fell in love, or at least, we acknowledged we were officially in love, though the actual feelings may have had earlier origins. Who knows how, why or when these things develop? (I am a train guy, not a love expert.) Perhaps the first inkling surfaced in the parched Australian Outback, maybe in rainy Ireland, maybe somewhere else. On an overcast spring morning, while reading the Sunday newspaper in our morning uniforms, Mindy in her pajamas, me in my sweatpants and a "Good Morning Viet Nam" t-shirt, Mindy asked the question of questions that lies like a time bomb below the surface of all unofficial couples.

"What are we doing?" If I had learned anything in my 60 years of existence, it was that this question must be treated seriously. Experience had taught me that this certainly didn't mean, "what are we going to do today?" But I was ready for it this time. I got down on my knees. I proposed in my sweatpants. We were married before a Seattle Municipal Court Judge on August 26, 2015, with our friends Mike and Caroline Ullmann as the sole witnesses to this historic event. Our wedding feast was a dinner for four at a nearby seafood restaurant on Lake Union.

What does this have to do with Trans-Canada train

travel? A lot, as it turns out. Since travel had been a big part of our lives, we began to talk about trips we would like to take—*together, like as a married couple.* My days of solo travel were over. I was in my sixties, and not getting any younger. The hardships I had endured in Finland— camping in the woods, trying desperately to pedal ahead of the next storm, talking to reindeer—were experiences I wasn't eager to duplicate. I now realized I enjoyed traveling up-class, and loved traveling with my friend, now wife. Mindy also liked to travel by train, a reason by itself for popping the question in 2015 to this lovely red-headed woman.

But there was another reason for changing my class of travel to one that involved less suffering. Since Finland, I had been diagnosed with cancer twice: first, in 2014, with prostate cancer—for which I underwent nine weeks of radiation therapy, which appeared to stop it—and then, in 2016, with colon cancer. This time the only viable cure was surgery to remove the part of the colon where the tumor had germinated. That procedure was successful. Follow-up lab results and other tests indicated that the cancer had not spread. Three months after the surgery I was hiking and biking again, the poster child for early cancer screening procedures. Returning to normal life was a gift, and yet I couldn't help but feel anxious about the future. These cancers had been detected when I was feeling good and in excellent physical condition. There had been no pain, no telltale sign that something was terribly wrong. Several

PSA tests, then a biopsy, had confirmed the prostate cancer. Two years later, a colonoscopy had detected the cancerous colon tumor. If nothing else, these twin traumas confirmed that life was indeed fragile. Once I was back on my feet, I decided it was time to stop thinking about retiring and to actually retire. I did that in 2017. Now I was ready for the rest of my life and I was determined to make it as interesting and happy as possible.

"You know," I said one night after dinner, when Mindy asked me if I wanted to do something special after my retirement, "I've been thinking about that trip we took in 2009. How much we enjoyed it, and how much we liked the dining car. If only the meals weren't so close together. If we traveled from East to West, we would gain an extra hour between meals. Maybe we should do the trip again, but this time go the other way."

Mindy was game, provided we got off and had time to explore. She wasn't interested in one continuous slog on rails. Neither was I. And that's how the Second Great Canadian Train Adventure came to be.

# CHAPTER 3

### Always Wanted to Take That Trip

WHENEVER I TELL SOMEONE that Mindy and I have traveled across Canada by train, their eyes brighten with interest. "I always wanted to do that trip," is the inevitable reply. The voice then trails off, as if my friend were wistfully recalling a long-lost unattainable love rather than a train trip across the broad shoulders of our big, friendly, reasonable neighbor to the north. The trip seems to be on everyone's bucket list, but rarely gets crossed off.

I have taken less attainable train trips. The *Trans-Siberian Express* was not an easy ticket to score for a solo journey in the dying days of the Soviet Union. I did that in 1987 and barely lived to tell the tale, experiencing a score of misadventures that I described in my first book, *The Gentleman from Finland—Adventures on the Trans-Siberian Express*. In the tally book of the ardent train traveler, the *Trans-Siberian* is Mount Everest. It is an eight-day continuous journey that starts in European Russia, crosses over the barely perceptible slopes of the Ural Mountains, bends around Lake Baikal, then finishes through the endless steppes of east Siberia, skirting the Amur River and terminating in Vladivostok. It's 5,625 miles long. No other passenger rail line is even close in length. Today, I suspect buying a ticket for the *Trans-Siberian* is easier, but a solo journey without the assistance of a tour guide, and perhaps a bodyguard, would still be a rail adventure out of the ordinary.

While the *Trans-Siberian* retains the glory of the longest passenger trip in the world,[2] the Trans-Canada, or *The Canadian,* as it is officially called, quietly resides in the number two position at 2,792 miles, barely edging out the *Indian Pacific*, which covers a span of 2,706 miles between Perth and Sydney, Australia. Number four is the *California Zephyr*, a journey Mindy and I took in 2010, which begins in Emeryville, California and ends in Chicago, three days and 2,438 miles later. I am not sure where the *Empire Builder* stands, yet another train Mindy and I have traveled with, but at 2,211 miles between Seattle and Chicago, I would think it ranks among the top ten.

What about the *Orient Express*? This *grande dame* of passenger railroad travel and the inspiration for an Agatha Christie novel was a luxury train that started operating between Paris and Istanbul in 1883. In modern times, however, it shared the fate of other passenger trains, gradually having its route shortened. Istanbul got whacked off as the final terminus in 1977, taking the "orient" out of "orient

---

2   The *Trans-Siberian Express* is the longest continuous passenger rail service in the world, according to the journal *Railway Technology*. A 2009 Wikipedia reference notes two longer lines, Moscow to Pyongyang and Kyiv to Vladivostok, though it is unlikely they are continuous or even still in operation given foreign border sensitivities. Any takers for a train trip to North Korea?

express" when the last stop was moved to Bucharest, then shortened again to Budapest. Finally, in December 2009, the *Orient Express* disappeared from the timetables forever. Other high-priced tourist trains replaced it, but let's be honest, these are not "real" passenger trains in that they offer regular service and are a means of transportation, not solely dedicated to tourism. Again, I was lucky enough to ride a segment of the old, albeit abbreviated, *Orient Express* in 1991, when I boarded in Zurich and rode to Budapest.

Heading into 2017, my collective train resume was looking fairly solid. I had recently retired from my job as Chief Financial Officer of the Kitsap County (Washington) Regional Library. I had plenty of time to knock off the *Indian Pacific* in Australia, and maybe even *The Ghan*, its sister train that bisects the Australian continent north–south, from Darwin to Adelaide. But there was something about the Canadian train that kept calling to me, as if there were unsettled business between us. I couldn't quite put my finger on it until one day it struck me like a bolt of lightning: the dining car. While Amtrak food has improved over the years, nothing has come close to the dining delight on wheels that so impressed us in 2009. These were real meals, with real silverware and table linens, that were somehow cooked to perfection as the train bucked through every kink in the single-track line. Mindy agreed. We needed to experience this epicurean delight, but this time instead of going from west to east, and having our mealtimes shortened by time zones, we would reverse direction and have the meal intervals lengthened by an hour each day. Brilliant. We congratulated each other. What a perfect way to celebrate my retirement. Australia, and the 14-hour plane flight to get there, could wait. *The Canadian's* dining car beckoned yet again.

There was just one last add-on, which became apparent when we looked at maps. Taking the train in both directions would be a little too much in terms of time and money (apparently frugality can never be completely eradicated), so we decided to fly east. We had already visited Toronto and Montreal by train on our previous trip. We were curious about what lay beyond: Nova Scotia, for example. Not only was Nova Scotia *terra incognita* for us, but Halifax was also the terminus for *The Ocean*, the last operating passenger train in the Maritime Provinces. *The Ocean* also has the distinction of being the oldest operating "named" train in North America, beginning service in 1904. It once operated daily, but now service has been reduced to three trains a week that make the overnight run to Montreal. From Montreal, we would connect with another train, a half day's journey, to Quebec City, another destination that intrigued us. With the start in Halifax, we would transverse the entire breadth of Canada by rail. For me personally, it would mean that I could claim to have traveled around the world—at least the portion north of the equator—by train, with a gap left to fill in central Europe.

We would have started our Canadian train odyssey in Newfoundland if that were possible, but we were 48 years too late. *The Caribou,* a passenger train that linked St. John's on the island's east coast to Port aux Basques on the west, was the world's longest narrow-gauge railroad at 906 miles. *The Caribou,* never known for its punctuality, was replaced by bus service in 1969.

# CHAPTER 4

### *The Ocean*

THE SPACIOUS HALIFAX TRAIN STATION, built in 1928, reminds me of the cliché about being all dressed up with nowhere to go. The colonnaded entry off Hollis Street leads to a spacious lobby. Off to one side is the entrance to the Westin Hotel, formerly the Nova Scotian. This was one of the grand hotels built by the Canadian National Railway to provide luxurious and convenient accommodations to its rail passengers. This station replaced an older, more ornate neoclassical structure that had been damaged beyond repair in the great Halifax munitions explosion of 1917.[3]

On this overcast Friday a few dozen passengers lounge quietly on wooden station benches, awaiting the 1:00 p.m. departure of *The Ocean*, the only passenger train that departs today from this once-busy station. Two musicians—one a middle-aged man with a shaved head, playing the keyboard, and the other a slender woman with close-cropped hair and a pixie smile, strumming a

---

3  On December 6, 1917 the SS *Mont-Blanc,* a French cargo ship loaded with munitions, collided with another vessel in Halifax harbor. The resulting fire triggered the largest manmade explosion ever recorded prior to the advent of the nuclear bomb. The blast leveled two square miles of Halifax, killed 2,000 people and injured 9,000. Sixty people were killed in the railroad station, most by the collapsed roof.

guitar—gallantly sing to the sparsely occupied benches. I am not sure why the station needs the big-screen monitors to post the lone departure; most of the screen is empty. The next *Ocean* doesn't leave for two days. Perhaps it's an optimistic gesture of the ever-more-distant hope that the halcyon days of train travel will return.

In the golden era of passenger train travel between the world wars, four passenger trains a day—*The Atlantic, The Ocean, The Scotian* and the *Maritime Express*—left the Halifax station for Montreal. Regional trains served other towns in Nova Scotia and New Brunswick. But the *grande dame* of the region's trains was *The Ocean*. In the 1960s, ridership declined as the highway network expanded and air travel became cheaper and more frequent. On the Friday we strolled into the station, *The Ocean* was the last passenger train operating in the Maritime Provinces.

Mindy and I find a seat in the spacious station and wait to board. Thirty minutes before departure, the first-class passengers are called to the ticket counter to check in. From what I can tell, there are about eight of us. At home, I had pre-printed our boarding passes. These are scanned. The clerk asks each of us to hold out our left hand. Bright blue plastic bracelets are snapped onto our wrists, like a jailer handcuffing a prisoner. These are remarkably similar to the band I wore recently when I was admitted to the hospital for colon surgery.

"I guess they want to know who the first-class passengers are?" I quip.

"I feel like I've been admitted to a mental hospital," observes my wife.

Check-in, including bracelet attachment, takes two minutes. The clerk motions to a door. She says we can now board the train, whose sleek curved rear end is visible through the windows. We wander down the long line of passenger cars, looking for car 1539. It is the third to the end, but the door is locked. There is no attendant. There doesn't appear to be anyone around. We are apparently the only passengers who want to board the train. With the exception of two eager beavers who are speed-walking far ahead of us, the other first-class passengers remain milling around the station as if in some weird hypnotic state induced by the bracelets. I wonder if I'm going to have to drive the train myself to Montreal. I shrug, and motion to Mindy to proceed. We walk on. The next car is also 1539, but it, too, is locked.

"Is this the right train?" asks Mindy. I can tell she is getting worried, wondering what sort of mess I have managed to get us into only five minutes into our big Canadian train adventure.

"Of course this is the right train. There are no other trains other than that single carriage parked on the next track" I reply, an air of fake confidence in my tone. Meanwhile, I am thinking: Could there possibly be another train? Perhaps an invisible one like in the Harry Potter movies?

We walk on. It is a long train. Was there an episode of

*Twilight Zone* that started like this? Please God, I don't want to run into Rod Serling at the end of the next car.

We finally reach a young attendant, who cheerfully waves us aboard yet another car 1539. We find room seven and wedge in the key, which looks like a thin rectangle of plastic Swiss cheese. I open the door to our home for the next 20 hours. The compartment consists of a long couch that is subdivided into two large seats. A third seat can be created by lowering the armrests between the two larger seats that bisect the couch. For sleeping, the couch transforms into a bunk. The second bunk folds down from near the ceiling. Opposite the couch is a small sink, with a mirror and a several cubbyholes. This also accommodates the world's thinnest closet, which is just big enough to hang a couple of threadbare shirts. A door leads to a separate chamber housing the toilet and sink. A strange metal T-bar juts from the rear of the commode. Its use is not readily apparent.

"What do you think that is for?" asks Mindy.

"I'm not sure" I say, equally puzzled by the contraption. "It looks like a T-bar on a ski lift. Maybe it's a grab-bar for those of us who do not always sit on the toilet."

We do our best to shoehorn our two suitcases and day-packs into our little rectangle. A few minutes after settling ourselves, Jessica, our attendant and the same woman who greeted us a few minutes earlier, pops in. She reviews the various safety features of the compartment, then shows us the call button for the attendant. She says she will put our bunks down when we go to dinner. This is fine with us.

"One more thing," she says. "Do you need the ladder to get into the top bunk?"

Mindy and I look at each other. We have traveled on a lot of overnight trains, so we have a tradition when it comes to sleeping arrangements. The tradition is this: Mindy, bless her heart, takes the top bunk because she tends to sleep more soundly and gets up less than me during the night. Among her other outstanding qualities, this might be one of major reasons why I married her. Here was someone who not only likes to travel by train, but also takes the top bunk without complaint—at least not much. What a deal! However, there is one important trade-off that makes this arrangement work. In the morning, the job of fetching two cups of hot coffee falls to the occupant of the bottom bunk. I have mastered the art of pouring coffee on a moving train, then balancing the cups as I make my way back to the compartment. I have yet to spill or inflict third-degree burns on myself. We then both relax with our morning coffee on the bottom bunk as the train rumbles on. It is a pleasant way to spend a morning on the move. This routine works very well on Amtrak Superliners. Each car is equipped with a coffee station on the upper floor. The coffee fetching is more challenging on the rare occasion when we are stuck with a first-floor compartment. That means negotiating a narrow stairway to the coffee station. Still, it's worth the trade-off.

"Do you use a ladder?" asks Mindy of Jessica, who is

young and appears to be in excellent physical condition.

"No, I just climb on up," she says, motioning to a few precarious small toeholds in the cubbyhole vanity opposite our couch.

"Okay, I don't think I need it," says my wife.

After Jessica leaves, I look at Mindy as if she has lost her mind.

"Are you crazy?" I say. "She's twentysomething; she probably backflips into bed. How are you going to get up there on a moving train? Show me the climbing path."

Mindy carefully examines the bunk. The mysterious footholds that Jessica alluded to have disappeared. "Maybe you're right," sighs my wife. "We don't want another incident."

———

Indeed, we do not. The incident Mindy refers to occurred on one of our frequent overnight trips on Amtrak's *Coast Starlight*, the train that links Seattle to Los Angeles. We board in Seattle. Twenty-four hours later, give or take an hour, we arrive in San Jose. My parents live in nearby Los Gatos.

On this particular evening, as the train headed to Klamath Falls in south central Oregon, Mindy gamely climbed into the upper berth of what Amtrak calls a "Roomette." I settled into the lower bunk. I heard the usual rustling around above me, then words of frustration. Then some thumping, followed by more words of frustration of the unprintable kind.

"Are you okay up there?" I asked.

"I'm stuck" came the reply.

"What do you mean you're stuck?"

"I climbed in the wrong way. I tried turning around, but now I'm stuck."

I got out of the bottom bunk and peered up into the upper bunk. Mindy had twisted herself into an impossible angle and was now wedged between the ceiling, the wall and the safety webbing that is designed to keep passengers from rolling out of bed and crashing into the floor. She looked like a fish snarled in a gill net, or a human pretzel.

"Maybe you should call the attendant," she said.

I had visions of the Jaws of Life being called for this unlikely emergency. Worse yet, I envisioned the next day's headlines in the Klamath Falls newspaper: "Amtrak Train Halted to Extract Woman Stuck in Upper Bunk." We don't need this. Not us, we are train people; we solve our own problems.

"Let me see if I can help before we do that," I proposed.

I managed to untangle her limbs. With me bracing her so she wouldn't fall out, she managed to pivot into the correct position. Afterwards, we had a good laugh, but also realized there is only one direction to properly slot yourself into the upper bunk. You have to get your head in the right direction, which has to be near the steps that are built into the compartment's furniture. Unless you're a midget or have retractable legs, it is almost impossible to turn around in the bed once you crawl in.

—

Meanwhile, back on *The Ocean* Mindy makes the wise decision to fetch Jessica and tell her that the ladder might be useful. She returns a few minutes later.

"Turns out Jessica is a gymnast, that's how she does it," says Mindy. "She told me no problem with the ladder. She'll put it up when she makes up the room."

Once we are settled, I grab the timetable, which is in the form of a booklet, showing the route and offering brief descriptions of some of the sights we will pass. Mindy gives me that look.

"I just want to read up on what we are going to see," I say, lamely.

"Ah hah," she replies, knowing that I can sometimes be obsessed with the schedule and whether we are on time.

One of the joys of train travel is that it frees you of obligation. You sit back and relax. Everything is taken care of. The rails will deliver you to your destination. I know of no train that has ever gotten lost. Nevertheless, taking a long-distance train trip requires some mental preparation. An overnight trip, such as the one we are about to undertake, is an ideal length because it's long enough to get into the rhythm of the trip, but short enough to ward off restlessness, though one might feel mushy-headed after the first night of fitful sleeping in a constantly-shifting bed. Longer trips, like *The Canadian*, are more challenging. I had managed to cross Russia on the *Trans-Siberian Express* in 1987, but it was a harrowing journey. Loneliness, sleep deprivation, endless vistas of the steppe every day, language barriers . . . all conspired to drive me to the brink of mental and physical exhaustion by the time the trip was over. This time, older, wiser and with a companion, I knew this trip would a snap. Yes, I had certain obsessions that would eventually emerge on a long train trip; don't we all? Mine is the need to endlessly consult the timetable and map to determine our position and whether we are on time. I would have made a great navigator or the director of Swiss Rail. This habit tends to drive my wife nuts. She wants me to relax, be calm, no need to worry about such things. And she is right to a point. After all, someone has to keep the train on schedule. But I guess that is the conductor's job, not mine.

On this trip, I vow to try and cure myself of this once and for all. What did it matter whether we were on time? We are retired. It's not like we have an important meeting with the Prime Minister. My wife, bless her, along with a succession of yoga teachers, stresses the concept of staying in the moment. This is the perfect mental state for train travel. I can invoke the moment by being keenly observant, appreciating each scene as it unfolds beyond our window. This will keep my mind occupied, give me greater appreciation of Canada, and hopefully crowd out such thoughts as: Are we on schedule? In my journal, I called this my Zen Train Mind.

I put the timetable back in its pouch. We're off to a good start, I think. Let the Zen Train Mind roll!

## CHAPTER 5

### Troubadours of the Tracks

I HAD ASSUMED, since *The Ocean* was scheduled to depart at 1:00 p.m., that lunch would not be served, yet another budget-cut victim to keep the operation rolling. Before arriving at the station, we stopped at a nearby grocery store and bought a couple of boxed salads and sandwiches to hold us until dinner. After we boarded, we were asked whether we wanted the early or later lunch sitting. That was a pleasant surprise, another reminder not to rely on assumptions.

Lunch call came before the train left the station. This dining car is a little different than others we have experienced. On one side of the aisle are tables for four, but on the opposite side are tables for two. The attendant ushers us to a table for four; I guess we're going to have company.

Moments later the duo who had been singing in the station lobby slide into the opposite seats. We introduce ourselves and discover we are sharing our lunch table with two accomplished songwriters and folk musicians.

Robert and Cailin are from Halifax. They are in the middle of their "2 of Hearts" tour, which has taken them to Germany and the Netherlands. They returned two weeks ago. Soon they will be playing throughout Nova Scotia and New Brunswick. In the meantime, they have received a grant to play aboard *The Ocean*. In exchange for a free round-trip train ride, they have agreed to play three 45-minute "concerts" aboard the train. The big rule is they can only perform songs by Canadian artists. A tip jar is also a no-no, but they can sell their CDs.

"Where are you going to play?" I ask.

"We're not sure," replies Robert. "They said they would let us know, but my guess is that it will probably be the lounge car."

Although the grant is bare-bones, Robert and Cailin were intrigued by the chance to perform their work as the train made its way through the lush Canadian countryside. Like us, the slow, relaxing pace of train travel appealed to them. Formerly from Vancouver, BC, they moved to Halifax several years ago, where they found the music scene more interesting and open to their folk style. Now they are in the process of downsizing, selling their house, and attempting to delve into their music passion full-time while traveling.

Robert is about my age, 62, and Cailin appears younger, though given her youthful appearance it is difficult to tell how much younger. From our conversation with them, I glean that they have lived together long enough to know what they want out of life. They have set a course for the next phase and are following it, beginning with the process of shedding the detritus of objects that accumulates in a lifetime. Now they are getting to the point where they are nimble enough to travel and play their music.

Mindy and I have also talked of downsizing. Our lives are punctuated by trips to Goodwill or other charities who might take our stuff. Collectively, we have a lot of stuff, but as we age it has dawned on us that we are not much interested in stuff as we are in experiences. It is much easier to haul around and store life experiences than a lot of extra furniture. Robert and Cailin are ahead of us in this regard, but we are all traveling in the same direction. This mindset is probably why we found train travel so appealing. Rather than being loaded into a metal cylinder, strapped into a narrow seat and told when it was okay to make a break for the bathroom, we can wander about the train at leisure, absorb the process of the journey and pee whenever we damn well please. Yes, it takes longer to get to your destination, but when time isn't scarce, who the hell cares? Besides, on a plane we would never have crossed paths with Robert and Cailin.

As we talk, I barely notice that *The Ocean* has eased out of the station and slowly begun making its way north through the Halifax suburbs. We soon traverse the vast open wetlands bisected by the meandering Shubenacadie River, whose nearly empty channel looks as if it had recently been filled with chocolate milk. This is the estuary of the upper Bay of Fundy, scene of some of the world's biggest tidal changes. The tide is out now.

"The tidal bore comes up those channels in a big wave," explains Robert, who has witnessed this phenomenon. "It's kind of fun to take a canoe or kayak and ride the bore upriver."

As we travel further north toward Truro, the land is laced with a myriad of lakes and rivers. Robert explains that in the days before the railroad and roads, traders would barge shipments from Nova Scotia's Atlantic Ocean side to the Bay of Fundy using the network of interconnecting rivers and lakes, portaging when necessary.

After bragging about the food on *The Canadian*, our lunch fare is disappointing. Mindy and Cailin barely touch their turkey tetrazzini. My meatloaf sandwich is weirdly encased in a ring of bacon. It looks like a giant hockey puck. I nibble at it, finding it rather tasty, but the sheer bulk is frightening for someone who has been warned about eating big portions of meat.

With lunch over, we bid Robert and Cailin goodbye and promise to attend their performance when announced. As we wobble back to our car, I look for a place where I can find coffee in the morning to fulfill my part of the bunk bargain. We find Jessica and learn that coffee is available six cars behind us in the lounge car, at the very end of the train. I have never negotiated a six-carriage traverse balancing two hot cups of coffee. I wonder how I can do this with the train heaving and hawing. But a deal is a deal.

Thank goodness my wife is reasonable. "You know you don't have to do that," she says.

"Thanks, I'll make it up to you on *The Canadian*."

*The Ocean* gains speed after a stop in Truro, a town known not only for its location on the Bay of Fundy but also as the home of the Stanfield Underwear Company. In case you didn't know, Stanfield invented the trap door on long johns.

By late afternoon, the scenery of marshy plains and lakes is replaced by hills with thick forests, bogs and thickets. It looks like perfect Moose habitat. Every few miles, a clearing emerges with a few log homes, all sporting enormous piles of firewood, some with moose antlers nailed above the front doors. After these settlements pass, the thick forest returns, interspersed with watery bogs sporting spindly trees that look as if they had drowned. We are glued to the window searching for the elusive moose when Robert, his keyboard tucked under his arm, pops his head into our cabin.

"We're going to play in the lounge car, which is the one before the dining car," he says. "See you there."

By the time we bob and weave through five cars, the pair is already performing. A few passengers sit in bright red lounge seats. Robert perches his keyboard on a counter, while Cailin stands to the side, guitar in hand. The mix of contemporary pop and folk is refreshing and seems suited to the train, though I am not sure how they manage to stay focused through the frequent announcements on the intercom.

As we are serenaded, the train rolls through Amherst,

Sackville and Moncton. These towns all feature uniformly well-kept houses with trimmed gardens and yards, stately churches and orderly streets. They are a picture of tranquility. One would think nothing bad has ever occurred in these places.

But, as I know from previous trips across Finland and Siberia, appearances can be deceiving. One aspect of train travel that I like is that it gives you time to observe, to contemplate and, in today's modern world, do a bit of research on the move. Even Canada, our big, friendly northern neighbor, has its unsavory moments in history. Moncton, a lonely stop for the train, where a few passengers board and even fewer depart, bears substantial historical significance, not all of it pleasant.

—

Before the coming of the Europeans, this was the territory of the Mi'kmak nation, a culture of hunters and gatherers. But in the early 1600s the Mi'kmaks were forced to share their dominion when settlers from France, who called the land Acadia, arrived, diking the Bay of Fundy tidal flats and transforming the bay-bed to farms. For the most part, the Mi'kmaks and the Acadians in relative peace. Then came the English and Scots, settling mostly in the south, in the area that became Halifax. The British were more interested in expanding the British Empire than in coexistence with the Mi'kmaks or Acadians. Acadian status worsened after 1710, the year the British gained full control of Nova Scotia. Not only were the Acadians now ruled by a foreign power, but they were cut-off from other French settlers who had established thriving colonies in Montreal and Quebec. This cultural isolation had linguistic consequences, as it virtually froze the Acadian French dialect in time. Today, French spoken here resembles the colloquial French of the seventeenth and eighteenth centuries.

Tension with the British boiled over in the 1750s during the French and Indian War. The British suspected the Acadians were allied with the French and the Mi'kmaks. Some were, but others tried to remain neutral. But neutrality didn't work after the British took Fort Beausejour, a French and Indian stronghold located not far from where *The Ocean* now passes. Among the defenders were Acadians, a revelation that only fed British paranoia that all Acadians were against The Crown.

What followed was one of those historic tragedies that, outside of present-day Acadian settlements, have largely become a historical footnote. Now known as the Great Deportation or the Great Expulsion, the British expelled nearly three-quarters of the Acadian population from Nova Scotia. Nearly 12,000 Acadian men, women and children were deported; about a third of these died during transport. Some were taken to France and others to the Caribbean islands, while still others were sent to the New England colonies to become indentured servants. More fortunate deportees, with the help of Spain, made their way to the

Louisiana territory, and their descendants became today's Cajun culture. In 1764, some nine years after the deportations began, the British allowed the Acadians to return, though they were not at first allowed to return to the areas they originally inhabited.

Today, major Acadian settlements are found in north Cape Breton. Other Acadians found their way back to Moncton, which is the largest Acadian-influenced city in Canada and home to New Brunswick's only French-language university. Ironically, the name Moncton is derived from Robert Monckton, the British commander who captured Fort Beausejour—the event that precipitated the Great Deportation.

—

Dinner is a vast improvement over lunch. We snag a table for two and soon are toasting the beginning of our train travel—Mindy with a Canadian red wine and me with a local microbrew. My entrée is seafood pasta, which includes fresh mussels, clams, lobster and shrimp, while Mindy has roast chicken. After dinner, we head to the lounge car at the end of the train, where Robert and Cailin gamely play their second performance for an audience of five, plus a couple of rambunctious children who are noisily concocting a hot chocolate solution at the back of the car. Robert plays with his back to the window, which shows the receding single-track we had just traveled. Big puffy clouds float across the sky, some trailing veils of rain that linger in the deep blue sky. A rainbow arcs over the forest, disappearing beyond a lake that comes into view. But still no moose.

# CHAPTER 6

### *The Ocean* Arrives

FOR ME, THE FIRST NIGHT ABOARD ANY TRAIN is always long and usually sleepless. It takes time to acclimate to the motion and rhythm of the carriage. Each train has its own cacophony of sounds. Mindy and I have ridden the *Coast Starlight* so many times we instinctively know the location of the rough tracks. *The Ocean* is a new experience, so the nuances are unfamiliar and take some getting used to. As I begin to drift off, an unpleasant odor permeates the cabin. Somewhere in north New Brunswick or southeast Quebec, *The Ocean* and a skunk had a chance encounter that didn't end well for the skunk; at least that's the story left by the lingering aroma that permeates our compartment in the middle of the night.

In my restless, sleepless state, my mind wanders from thought to thought. First I am in Finland, painfully pedaling through the silent forest in the rain. But then my mind jumps again, settling on the fresher trauma of my colon cancer diagnosis. Had it spread? How many surgeries would I require? What about this extra sack that would be attached to my intestine to shunt the waste away from the healing lower intestine? I did not look forward to wearing and maintaining this external septic tank. Surgery day came. My dominating thought was that if I managed to survive reasonably intact Mindy and I were going to do something fun—big fun—when I recovered.

—

I'll never forget easing out of unconsciousness to chaos, a memory permanently etched into my brain. The patient in the next bed was screaming. Nurses and orderlies attempted to soothe him, telling him he was in the recovery room, not hell. He didn't believe them. The commotion only temporarily distracted me from the pain in my abdomen. A nurse attending to my distressed neighbor saw that I was stirring and walked to my bed. She asked if I was in pain. I nodded. She adjusted the spigot from one of several tubes emerging from my arm. Relief was almost instantaneous. Sensing that the commotion across the aisle distressed me, she volunteered that sometimes when patients come out of anesthesia, they are psychotic. Fortunately, that was not me. But that didn't mean I wanted to linger in post-op; I wanted out of that insane asylum as soon as possible. I tried to sit up to feel where my new appendage was located, but the pain stopped me. From my prone position, I couldn't detect anything unusual. At least they hid it well, I thought.

At last, an orderly and a nurse came to wheel me away. Once again I was in motion. Okay, I wasn't on a train, but I was moving and that made me happy. I rolled into a sunlit corridor on smooth well-centered wheels, like the cushioned ride of a Swiss train. They are taking me to a good place, location known, schedule set. Enjoy the ride. And I did enjoy the short journey because I thought it would lead to longer, better journeys in the future. I just needed to stop at the next station to rest and heal for a few days. I was wheeled into my room, where Mindy, all smiles, waited.

"I just talked to Dr. Kratz," she told me. "The surgery went very well. And guess what, sweetie, you don't have a bag. Dr. Kratz said the portion of colon that was removed can heal without the bypass. Yahoo!"

Talk about a get-out-of-jail card! Later tests revealed that the cancer had not spread. That did it for me: I was retiring, then we were going to take that long train trip.

———

Now, as I contemplate the dancing shadows on the wall of the train compartment, I feel a sense of fulfillment for keeping my post-operation vow. I eventually drift off. When I awake, *The Ocean* is backing slowly over the Quebec Bridge, the longest cantilever span in the world. Below are the broad blue waters of the Saint Lawrence River. I check my watch. It is after 6:00 a.m. We have just left Sainte-Foy, the gateway to Quebec City. The back-up maneuver is necessary to get the train back to the cut-off from the main line, which parallels the south shore of the

Saint Lawrence. Sainte-Foy is on the north shore.

Sainte-Foy presented a challenge when planning the trip. Our ultimate destination is Quebec City, a tantalizing 12 miles away. But we are not getting off. When booking the trip, I couldn't see slogging off the train at six in the morning, shuttling to Quebec City, then waiting several hours for our hotel room to be ready. No, not us, we are retired. We are train people. We stay to the end. We are also breakfast and coffee people. Clearly, the lesson of my newfound Zen Train Mind philosophy—to relax and enjoy—applies here. We thought it best to take *The Ocean* to its terminus at Montreal, then double back on a local train, arriving back in Quebec City at about 3:00 p.m., in time to check into our hotel. But this back-and-forth game does gnaw at my sense of efficiency, an issue that Zen Train Mind may not cover. It's just plain irritating to be on a train that is moving backwards. In my morning stupor I compose a mental letter to VIA suggesting some minor schedule alterations.

*Dear Yves Desjardin-Siciliano,*
*VIA President and Chief Executive Officer:*

*First, I congratulate you on the excellent VIA train service between Halifax and Montreal. Keeping this system running must be a supreme challenge. Second, In the spirit of keeping passenger rail travel alive in the Maritime provinces, I would like to offer a few humble, yet visionary, suggestions that might* serve to boost ridership and keep at bay those who would rather see this train in a museum than on an actual working rail line.

A. My wife and I were disappointed not to see a moose, given that the region we bisected contains one of the largest concentrations of the ungainly ungulate in the world. If you could guarantee a moose sighting on every trip you would fill carriage 1539 and its cousins to the brim every trip. But how? At first, I thought a mechanical moose could be hidden underground in a missile silo-like structure near one of New Brunswick's many charming swamps. When the train approaches, the engineer could flip a switch, causing the moose to rise into position. After the train passes, the moose could be lowered back into the silo. On reflection, I realized that maintenance and operation costs of this contraption would probably be shouted down by the same back-bench budget-busting troglodytes who doomed your sister trains while starving The Ocean down to three trips a week. A less costly idea would be to recruit part-time employees to dress in a moose suit and station themselves near an approaching train. I realize outreach would be necessary to warn neighborhood hunters of the imposter moose. I might *suggest Kevlar as an inner coating to the moose suit; you know, just in case the outreach program doesn't reach everyone.*

A. *One of the prime destinations of The Ocean is Quebec City. But the current schedule has the train arriving at the Sainte-Foy Station at 6 am, an ungodly hour for the many senior citizen tourists who ride your train. I realize complicated factors involve train schedules, but in the interest of offering out-of-the box suggestions for improvement I toss this out for your consideration. How about leave Halifax at 5 pm and arrive in Sainte-Foy at 10 am? In fact, forget about the whole backing out of Sainte-Foy business; just stop the train opposite of Quebec City and fling passengers across the Saint Lawrence via giant catapults. Outgoing passengers would land in special nets on the opposite shore near the Hotel Le Chateau Frontenac. Of course, we would need to work out stuff like trajectory and speed, but those are mere details. (We're train people and train people are big idea people!) Advertise it as a VIA adventure travel package, like zip-lining across the Saint Lawrence (except with no line but lots of zip). I think that would help boost interest among millennials, who are always looking for new experiences. For geezers like me, have fresh croissants and coffee waiting at the other end. That's all I need and a loo, too.*

*Humbly Yours,*
*R.M. Goldstein, Retired Public Servant*

Letter composed, I roll over and go back to sleep. When I awake, we are again rolling in the correct direction, up the Saint Lawrence's south shore, and making a beeline for Montreal.

The train arrives in Montreal three hours later, almost exactly on time, stretching our streak of VIA on-time arrivals to two in a row. What's more, Mindy has been spared my usual shenanigans of schedule and timetable checking. We wait a couple of hours in the busy and well-appointed station, then board our train back to Quebec City, traveling the same route we came by in the morning. That's what train people do; that's also what people who don't like to get up at six in the morning do. By midafternoon we revisit Sainte-Foy, but this time continue the final 12 miles, skirting the old city to the north before pulling into the Gare du Palais, a vintage 1915 architectural masterpiece that resembles a miniature Chateau Frontenac.

### Interlude

This is a book about traveling across Canada by train. You might have noticed we are only a quarter of the way across this extremely long country. Why are we stopping here?

I will return both to the newfound Zen Train Mind one of the participants has discovered and to the actual trip itself in a moment. But in fulfilling my promise to plan a trip that features some "get offs", we did spend a splendid six days in Quebec City. We strolled through the old city many times, ate in its restaurants and visited its museums, and even took in a session of the provincial Parliament. We did not stay at the Hotel Le Chateau Frontenac, as apparently there are still some limits to my conversion to first-class accommodations (although that could change the next time I'm along this route if VIA adopts my catapult idea).

As you may have noticed in the first part of this narrative, I have proudly referred to my wife and myself as "train people."[4] I suppose true train people would have taken the train back to Montreal, then to Toronto to make the connection with *The Canadian*. But in the interest of time, we flew (gasp!) from Quebec City to Toronto. Let the record show that both of us have trained between Toronto and Montreal (2009) and, as described in the previous chapter,

---

4  I make the distinction between "train people" and "trainspotter" (sometimes referred to as a "foamer"). Trainspotters can be seen frequently hanging off bridges photographing passing trains. They have the uncanny ability to cite the manufacturer, horsepower and piston position of every steam locomotive manufactured. The details of a train's composition (called a consist, by the way), its pedigree and exact dimensions of its couplings are of intense interest. In contrast, train people like to ride in the train and look out the window. They could care less whether it is being pulled by a General Electric diesel or a ham sandwich. Once on an Amtrak trip, Mindy and I found ourselves seated at lunch across from a retired Amtrak engineer. I said that I liked to ride on trains and would like to ask him a question. "You're not a foamer are you?" he asked, alarm in his voice. I assured him no, but I did have a question about whether there was a bathroom in the engine cab. What happens if the engineer must pee? I always thought this might explain many of the unexplained stops Amtrak trains sometimes make. Unfortunately, the answer to the question has become the victim of a faulty memory.

trained between Montreal and Quebec City. I still like to think we are train people despite this one transgression in the interests of time. Failure to double back cannot be a disqualifying action. No way! If it's any consolation, I can report that Toronto's Pearson International Airport is now connected to downtown Toronto by a dedicated high-speed rail line. The last stop is Union Station, the location of our departure the next day and across the street from the Royal York, where we were booked for the night. That's right, first class all the way baby!

# CHAPTER 7

### First Night Aboard *The Canadian*

THE TRANQUILITY OF THE VIA LOUNGE is interrupted by a rustling, like the approach of a distant storm. The sound comes from the Great Hall. The commotion grows louder. Like nervous prairie dogs scenting danger, the few passengers in the lounge perk up their heads from books and magazines.

The lounge doors bang open. In surges a sea of aged humanity, pulling big suitcases and shouldering bulky daypacks. Some sport canes, a few are in wheelchairs, and one wizened man pushes a caddy with a pair of oxygen tanks strapped to it. They gather near the entrance like a swarm of bees clustering around a new hive. The cluster grows until a harried-looking young man toting a clipboard enters the room. He threads his way to the front of the crowd.

"Try to find seats in here," he says, then glances at his clipboard.

"When do we get our train tickets!" shouts a woman in the back.

"I will distribute your tickets right now," replies the trip leader in a tone that suggests that if he delays a minute longer he might be trampled.

Another, a short man sporting a "Save Pluto" baseball cap, shouts: "When can we eat!"

The trip leader, now busy distributing tickets to the horde while crossing off names from his clipboard, looks up with a startled expression. "Right. food," he mutters, then turns and announces, "If anyone wants to eat dinner before we leave, I will escort you to Longos (Longos is a cross between Whole Foods and a supermarket with deli take-out). We won't have much time, so please do not wander off."

Members of this Grand Circle Tour spread into the lounge like an occupying army. As soon as that tour group distributes itself, another, smaller, tour group starts a new cluster near the entrance. These travelers are of the same demographic but are a little fitter. We later learn this is a Road Scholar (formerly called Elderhostel) group. They appear to be in a less agitated state, probably because they have been fed and have tickets in hand.

Thirty minutes before the scheduled departure, VIA staff usher us through the train station, down a labyrinth of stairs and onto the platform, where the carefully restored 1950s-era silver carriages gleam in the fluorescent lights of the underground burrow. Because the train is long, the boarding gate for passengers near the front of the train is different from those near the rear.

Mindy and I find Car 110, the nameplate "Thompson

Manor" prominently displayed on the carriage's side. Compartment F is spacious, the upper and lower beds already down, beds made. During the day, usually while passengers are at breakfast, the carriage steward comes, folds up the beds and sets up two executive-style chairs that face the window. That is the day configuration. Unlike the Amtrak trains, where the seats are built into the carriage, the chairs in *The Canadian's* sleeper can be rearranged. On our previous trip, Mindy and I arranged our chairs so we looked straight out the window.

Opposite the bunks are a sink, a mirror and various cubbyholes to stash toiletries. Next to that, on the side caddy-corner to the window, is the door to the toilet. On the wall, adjacent to the sink, hangs a framed picture of a pair of sheep nuzzling each other. The title placard calls this work "Untitled" but below that is "Prince Edward Island," which, ironically, is the only province besides Newfoundland not served directly by a VIA passenger train. Given the culinary excellence of *The Canadian's* dining car, I wonder if "Lamb Chops" might be a more fitting title. But seriously, with the scarcity of real estate on the train, it seems VIA is missing out on a splendid opportunity to tout the wonders of the natural world that its rail lines witness. How about a photo of the snow-covered Rockies, Quebec City's Hotel Le Chateau Frontenac, or the mighty Saint Lawrence choked in winter ice? I wonder if another letter to management is in order, but I am quickly diverted from that idea by more pressing matters.

We stash our bags and organize ourselves for sleep, thankful to be rid of the mayhem in the lounge. However, our tranquility is soon interrupted by a loud knock upon our cabin door.

"The Raven," I grouse. "Nevermore!"

"Now what?" grumbles Mindy. It has been a long day of sightseeing in Toronto by foot. We are tired.

The carriage steward pops her head around the sliding door. This is Kristin, yet another cheerful, fit and young VIA employee. She will accompany us for the first half of the journey, to Winnipeg.

"I've asked some of the other passengers in the nearby compartments to join us in your room so I can give the safety and pre-boarding talk to everyone at once."

She motions into the corridor. Two women, perhaps a mother-daughter combination, crowd into our entryway, along with an elderly couple.

Kristin explains how the windows can be popped out in an emergency. The elderly couple appear perplexed by this explanation. They seem to think this is the normal way to leave the train, to jump out the window. Or, maybe they think Kristin wants them to jump off the train now. "No, no," says Kristin. "Only for EMERGENCIES." She pauses a bit to make sure this point hits home. Satisfied, she continues, pointing to a couple of white, doorbell-like buttons in the compartment. "Those are to call the attendant. There is also one in the bathroom that people always confuse for the flush button. It is not the flush button.

The flush is near the back of the seat." I am already envisioning a journey punctuated by many false bathroom emergencies.

Next is an explanation of the dining car, which is attached to Thompson Manor. On *The Canadian*, there are three reservation times for lunch and three for dinner. This is a train, after all, a full train as it turns out. One just doesn't waltz into the dining car and ask for a private table for two. The need to feed a lot of passengers requires organization and efficient use of space. The tables accommodate four, which means if you are a party of one, two or three you will likely break bread with strangers. First-time dining car passengers might find this awkward, but it is a good way to meet fellow travelers, many of whom you will be sharing the same narrow corridors with. Over the course of a few days a sense of community develops. This is one of the more magical aspects of long-distance train travel.

Beyond the dining car is the fabled dome car. In the lower deck, coffee, tea and fruit are available all day. There is also a small bar. Stairs lead to the upstairs dome, an excellent place to watch the scenery pass.

"I think the dining car attendant took reservations for tomorrow while you were in the waiting room, if not, he will come by soon to take care of you," says Kristin. We all nod. For us, reservations are in hand. We grabbed the prime middle seating between 6:00 p.m. and 7:00 p.m. Our experience as train people is already paying dividends.

"Breakfast is first-come, first-serve," continues Kristin.

One of the Grand Circle ladies raises her hand, as if she is at school asking the teacher a question.

"Can we eat after that?"

"After 8:30 the dining car is closed," Kristin replies. "It doesn't reopen until lunch."

The woman looks distressed, as if realizing a critical supply line will be cut off. She raises her hand again.

"How do you get to the dining car?"

"It's next door," replies a patient Kristin.

"But how?"

I glance at Mindy. We probably had the same thought. Have these people ever been on a train before? Do they think they jump across an open coupling like in the old western movies?

"You walk," replies Kristin, the smallest hint of frustration creeping into her voice.

"It's just down the hallway; press the button on the door, and there it is. You can't miss it," I chime in, trying to be helpful while also attempting to move these interlopers from our sleeping quarters.

The woman eyes me suspiciously. She's probably thinking: Who the hell do you think you are, Mister Know-It-All?

As the group shuffles out, I overhear the same woman who was mystified about how to get to the dining car grumble to her companion: "Their compartment is bigger than ours. I thought they were all the same."

When the gaggle leaves, I turn to Mindy.

"That woman was right. Our compartment is bigger."

"What?" says Mindy. "How are they not the same size? That chick was just jealous because we are so well organized."

I had booked the trip as early as the reservation system would allow. When I reached VIA by phone, the service representative asked me which compartment I wanted.

"Aren't they all the same?" I asked.

"That's what you would think," she replied. "But for some reason, on *The Canadian* compartment F is a little bigger than the others. People who have taken this train before always request compartment F."

Compartment F was still open. I booked it. It pays to be early.

# CHAPTER 8

## Zen Train Mind

MINDY IS TIRED. She climbs the ladder to her spacious upper bunk and is asleep in a matter of minutes. I should go to bed too, but the start of a long train ride still excites me. I have reacted this way since childhood, beginning with my first trip on the *Coast Starlight*. On those journeys, I was so mesmerized by the passing scenery that my parents thought my nose would permanently stick to the window. Later, they took me on short trips aboard the commuter trains that linked San Jose and San Francisco.

I am not sure why I was so fascinated by train travel. Was it the movement, the sounds? I remember the conductor's shout of "all aboard," the double wail of the train whistle and the gradual clanging of steel wheels on iron rails that signaled the start of what was always a magical journey for me—my own version of *The Hogwarts Express*.

Today there is no shout of "all aboard" and the rhythmic clickety-clack is gone, as today's rails are welded smooth. To be aware that the train is moving you must be aware of the silent, almost imperceptible movement forward that gradually increases in velocity. The station platform recedes, then disappears.

At night, in a big city, glimpses of life pass as the train slowly pushes its way through the dark. We pass an apartment. In a window, I see a man and woman sitting down for dinner. A few hundred feet later, in another building, a man stares at his computer. On another floor, a woman in a nightgown abruptly closes the bedroom curtain. The train moves on and so does life. You have the rare opportunity to observe, to contemplate, or do nothing because you have no need to do anything. You are free of obligation.

About 30 minutes after departure, *The Canadian* and a skunk have an untimely meeting. Not again, I think. In my construction of Zen Train Mind, I had not contemplated focusing on unpleasant odors for prolonged periods. But I will try. Indeed, this has been a rough couple of weeks for skunks crossing Canadian railroad tracks. Five minutes later we grind to a stop. Is the crew going to scrape the skunk off the wheels? With a lurch, the train starts again, backwards. We retrace our way back across the freeway that connects Toronto with its airport. We continue in reverse for 20 minutes, then stop and restart in reverse. Did we leave someone behind at Longos? Are we going back to fetch them? Did we miss a switch? There is no announcement. In the dark, amid strange surroundings, with the scent of skunk lingering, it is hard to know where we are. But it seems to me we are switching onto another track. No, this is not the way of Zen Train Mind. These are the wrong questions. I clearly need to refocus my effort. I shouldn't really care that the train is going backwards or about its rate of speed, which incidentally, for the record, is very slow. In the true abstract of Zen Train Mind, I probably am not even on a train, because that is only what I perceive in my current incarnation. I might be on a camel in Mongolia. I might be on a Greyhound bus full of dancing cats.

Maybe I'm taking this too far. Calm down! Concentrate on the journey as it is! Earth to Bob. . . .

Almost an hour after departure, the train halts again. Slowly, almost reluctantly, it begins to creep forward on the long journey to the West Coast. I can now go to bed knowing we are safely heading in the right direction.

# CHAPTER 9

### Rupert's Land

THE FIRST NIGHT DOESN'T GO WELL. In the fuzzy consciousness between sleep and wakefulness, I am vaguely aware of the train starting and stopping. I don't think I am dreaming, but I am not quite sure. In my semiconsciousness, I feel the train gain speed, a lot of speed. We should be pushing north through the densely populated neck of land between Lake Huron and Lake Ontario. In the dead of night, we will skirt the coast of Lake Huron, the only vista of the great lakes available on this last remaining transcontinental route, before heading inland toward Sudbury.

The lurching and swaying of the carriage rolls me in my bunk. On big lurches, I bump against the compartment wall. I think the engineer is mad because he's had to spend half the night scraping skunks off the wheels or on sidings waiting for freight trains to pass. Now, he's hellbent on making up time.

When I awake at seven, the train is perfectly still. I worm my way around my cozy bunk and peer out the window and am greeted by the sight of thick forest. Urban Canada is now far behind us. Mindy sits nearby, staring out the window. She is an early riser. She appears to be in the perfect Zen Train Mind pose, looking out the window, appreciating the scene for what it is, not concerned whether we are moving or not. I envy that.

"How long have we been sitting here?" I ask.

"We were here when I got up, and that's been awhile," she replies calmly. My wife usually rises at 5:30. "It seems like we were stopped most of the night."

"Yeah, I think that's right, though I had this dream where the train was going really fast and I was being bounced all over the place. I thought the engineer was pissed because of all the stops."

"I don't think that was a dream," replies Mindy dryly. "Either that, or we both had the same dream."

And with that exchange, *The Canadian* begins to creep forward, gradually gaining speed.

Where are we? I grab the map from the little holder by the side of my bunk. Have we reached Rupert's Land? Mindy rolls her eyes. After 40 years of friendship and a year of marriage, she knows me well. I need to know where I am. I attribute this to a genetically programmed instinct that clicks in when I am traveling, particularly on a train, though the phenomenon also occurs in cars and, with the advent of seat-back viewing screens, on airplanes. On a train, one *must* have a timetable and a map. Without these indispensable tools of the control freak, I become merely a Nervous Nellie, furtively glancing about, not sure where I am. You might ask: What about the global positioning device on a smartphone? And I would say to you, Mister Wise Guy, that we are in upper Ontario; here, there is no cell phone service, nada (at least, not on my el cheapo phone plan). All of this, of course, is mumbo-jumbo in the context of Zen Train Mind thought. A true Zen Train Mind adherent would not care about time or schedule. She would be in the moment, contemplating the scene out the window, noting its beauty, stillness and its overall sense of being. But I am not that person yet. I have much to learn on this trip.

The single-track right-of-way parallels no road. It cuts a solitary path through a wilderness of scrawny spruce and aspen, lakes and muskeg. Beaver dams abound. Sometimes the view changes to great swaths of dead trees, desolate white tree skeletons, perhaps drowned from the swampy conditions, killed by some bug or poisoned by acid rain. We pass tiny settlements consisting of cabins or dilapidated houses. One village sports a tiny one-room white A-frame with a sign in front that says, "Hudson's Bay Co."

~

Is this tiny cabin the last symbol of a trading company that was once the world's largest landowner? The transfer of Rupert's Land to Canada by the Hudson's Bay Company (HBC) in 1869 was the key event that eventually led to the creation of the Dominion of Canada, and ultimately to the building of a transcontinental railroad to link its far-flung provinces. But none of this would have happened if not for *Castor canadensis*, the North American beaver, one of the world's largest rodent species, with its buckteeth, flat tail and habit of felling trees, damming streams and creating wetlands. In the seventeenth century, beaver pelts were prized in Europe. They were the raw material for fashionable hats and other clothing accessories among the rich. Europeans had hunted their native beavers to extinction. A new source was needed. Canada and the northern United States were teeming with beavers waiting to be discovered by some enterprising explorer.

That person was Pierre-Esprit Radisson, a native-born French Canadian, whose unique background shaped him as a future North American explorer. Radisson was 17 when he was captured near Trois Rivieres (in modern-day Quebec) by marauding Iroquois, who soon realized they had someone special in their custody, a man-boy of exceptional courage, intelligence and resourcefulness. Adopted into the tribe, he fled, was recaptured, tortured and finally escaped again. He eventually made his way to New York—then a Dutch colony—and then to Europe, returning six years later on a ship with his brother-in-law Médard Chouart des Groseilliers with the goal to explore west of modern-day Quebec (then called New France). Radisson knew from his previous contacts with the Indians that these lands were rich in beaver. Permission was required, in this case from the King of France, whose governor in Quebec ruled New France. But the French were more concerned about British wresting control of the Saint Lawrence River, the colony's main transportation artery, from the mother country. If news got out that there were beavers galore to the west, the British would surely attempt to take the river and the colony. Who needed that? Permission was denied.

Radisson and Groseillers went anyway.

They returned to France with ships laden with furs and new knowledge of the land to the west. Instead of being hailed as heroes, they were arrested and fined. The cargo was confiscated. After release, the two explorers concluded the French wouldn't know a good deal if it hit them over the head. They next courted Boston businessmen, who saw profit in the idea and financed another expedition to northern Canada. That failed when the expedition ship got stuck in ice in the Hudson Straits. The two hard-luck explorers eventually landed in London, but the Great Plague beat them there. The Crown's movers and shakers, fearing plague-carrying rats, had fled the city. The pair waited for two years before attracting the attention of Prince Rupert, who saw potential in the venture. He convinced his cousin, King Charles II, to provide two ships, the *Eaglet* and the *Nonsuch*, for yet another expedition to Canada. The *Eaglet* was forced to turn back, but the *Nonsuch* completed the journey, returning with a hold full of beaver pelts.

That sealed the deal. King Charles II granted Prince Rupert and 17 others, mostly royalty and wealthy merchants, a royal charter creating "The Company of Adventurers of England Trading into Hudson's Bay," later to become known as the Hudson's Bay Company. The charter covered nearly one-third of North America, ranging from the coast of Labrador north to Hudson Bay and west to the Great Plains. Prince Rupert was appointed governor of what would become known as "Rupert's Land." Ironically, Radisson, whose discovery was not enough to overcome his low caste, was cut out of the deal, though a couple of hundred years later a hotel chain expropriated his name.

In the early 1800s, the territory expanded to include what is now British Columbia, Oregon, Washington and Northern California. The charter granted the company powers to administer justice, raise its own army and navy, build forts and declare war on non-Christian peoples. In return for this monopoly of power and potential wealth, Charles asked only that visiting royalty be presented with a pair of beavers and elk, live ones, a provision that was forgotten until 1927. That's when an Alberta rancher, Charles Allen, a member of the company's governing committee, uncovered the charter's original rent provision. He asked the visiting Prince of Wales (the future Edward VIII) where he wanted to stow his beavers and elk. The Prince diplomatically suggested that tanned skins and mounted heads would do just fine. On a visit on in 1970. Queen Elizabeth II received two live beavers, which she donated to the Winnipeg zoo.

For two hundred years, the Hudson's Bay Company, with its vast network of trading posts, flourished. Thanks to the ban on settlement imposed by the company to protect its trade franchise, Canada's west was relatively free of the bloody conflicts between Indians and settlers that afflicted the United States. But the discovery of gold in British Columbia in 1858 changed everything. Thousands of miners poured into British Columbia, and demand for furs waned. Political pressure mounted for the Canadian colonies to unite into a self-governing confederation.

In the late 1860s, amid demands to settle the west and declining profits, the company sought to sell its territory back to Great Britain. The British didn't want it. The United States, fresh from its Alaska territory purchase, offered to buy. In 1869, the company transferred the land to the new Dominion of Canada, which had been created in 1867 from the provinces of New Brunswick, Nova Scotia, Quebec and Canada (modern day Quebec and Ontario). There was only one problem; the new Dominion was broke. It had to borrow 300,000 pounds from Great Britain to compensate the company for Rupert's Land. Within a few years, Manitoba and British Columbia joined the Dominion, leading to pressure to link the new nation via a transcontinental rail line.[5]

---

5   The Hudson's Bay Company operates its own department stores in Canada. It also owns Saks Fifth Avenue.

# CHAPTER 10

### Ghost Moose

MINDY AND I ARE GLUED TO THE WINDOW. Perhaps in tribute to the land Radisson trod, we see signs of beavers: huge mounds of sticks clogging small rivers and creating swamps. It also looks like a perfect place to see a snacking moose in this province where the moose population has declined about 20 percent over the last decade. At last count, an estimated 92,300 are still wandering around. This should provide us with a better-than-even chance of spotting one. But none of the big ungulates come into view.

My second priority is to check on the availability of the shower, located just outside our cabin a few feet down the corridor. I slip out of our compartment, seeing from the corridor window that *The Canadian* is passing another large lake.

"There's a moose!" shouts a passenger, who has taken a moose observation position at the other end of the corridor. I look and see a solitary moose, standing on the shore, as if posing for a post card. Mindy pops out and thinks she catches a glimpse before a grove of trees blocks the view. The lake and moose are gone.

"I think it was a fake moose," says my wife.

"Maybe it's two guys in a moose suit," I respond. Mindy doesn't know about my moose suit idea. In fact, nobody does because the letter is still in my brain.

"Very funny," says my wife, who is not amused. Time to head for the shower.

By now *The Canadian* is 400 miles from Toronto. We have finished our northbound advance. The tracks now bend northwest through the wilderness of upper Ontario, where surely the beavers still outnumber humans.

Later in the day, the train slows and pulls into the town of Foleyet, another in a long line of wilderness whistle-stops for *The Canadian*. If your stop is Foleyet, Oba, Elsas, Gogama or any other of the numerous tiny settlements along the route, you need to provide advance notice to VIA. Otherwise, the train rolls on. Without train service, getting in and out of these tiny settlements requires hours of driving (if there is a road and it is open in the winter), flying by floatplane (if there is a lake) or a very long hike (if there is a trail). Though *The Canadian* is popular with tourists, it still serves as a vital transportation lifeline to these remote settlements.

We learn from Claire, the train's activities leader, via the public address system that the forest around Foleyet, a town built near the turn of the century by the railroad, is the haunt of the ghost moose, so named because it is white. The head of an unlucky one is mounted in a

Foleyet restaurant, a victim of an oncoming train in 1998. This squib of information leaves more questions than it answers. Is the ghost moose a genetic freak like the revered spirit bears of Vancouver Island, or did it fall into a vat of white paint?

It turns out that the ghost moose is not the product of a rare gene, but the indirect result of global warming. Because the winters are warmer than they once were, ticks no longer die off in the freeze. The little pests survive the winter by hopping onto a passing moose, then burrowing into its warm fur. Further accommodation is provided by an ample supply of moose blood. Agitated by the burgeoning population of tiny freeloaders, the moose tries to shed the ticks by rubbing against trees. This shears its brown topcoat, leaving the white root hairs exposed. Moose with a bad tick problem lose up to three-quarters of their brown fur and a fair amount of blood. Without its thick brown coat, a moose may not survive the winter.

This is not just a Canadian problem; reports of ghost moose have also appeared in the United States, prompting fish and game authorities in Idaho to warn hikers and hunters to stay clear of white-furred moose. They likely will be angry and will vent their anger on the first living thing they see.

After Foleyet, the train passes more spindly spruce, with dead lower branches shaped like a witch's broom. The land looked healthier eight years ago when we passed going in the opposite direction. I wonder if the swamps, with the skinny trunks of trees poking out like telephone poles, have something to do with warm winters. I begin to question my hypothesis that the myriad mounds of sticks are the work of beavers. Now, I think they may be fallen branches from the dying trees that get pushed together during high water. During the stops for freight trains, I look for the chewed pointed ends of sticks and logs that would indicate they have been felled by a beaver. I see no pointed ends here.

Something else is not quite right. In a land with endless lakes and marshes, we have observed only a handful of birds, and not a single duck. Mindy and I compare notes. Our list is not impressive: a raven, two Canada geese and a hawk.

We pull into Hornepayne, population 980. I see the old brick railroad station that we walked around in 2009. At about that time, some hopeful artist had tried to brighten the building with colorful murals of daily life. But today the building looks as decrepit as ever, a relic waiting to collapse. The murals are as faded as thousand-year-old frescoes found in Roman ruins. Located in the middle of the boreal forest, Hornepayne owes its existence to the Canadian National Railroad, but it has also spawned several National Hockey League players and has been considered a prime location for burying nuclear waste because of its isolation. Meanwhile, the population dwindles, down another 70 since my last visit and almost 700 in the last 25 years.

This is one of our longer stops. After observing the decaying station, we resume our exercise routine of marching the length of the train, then back to the carriage. Before I reboard, I ask Kristin if she thinks the train will fall further behind schedule. I note that we are now about an hour and twenty minutes behind.

"We always lose time on this stretch, but we almost always make it up at night," she says cheerfully.

"We'll see," I mumble under my breath as I climb aboard, realizing that I have again violated one of the tenets of Zen Train Mind. I need to celebrate the existence of Hornepayne and honor the miracle of its perseverance, and to quit worrying about the train's tardiness. A few miles outside Hornepayne we pull over yet again for another freight train.

Dinner does not disappoint. My prime rib is as tender and juicy as I remember from our last trip on *The Canadian,* when I ordered it on the second night of our eastbound journey. Mindy orders cod, which she declares excellent. Our seatmates are Pat and Holly, the mother-daughter combination from Rochester, New York, who we first met at the beginning of the trip during the safety lecture. They belong to the Grand Circle Tour. Pat tells us that they will disembark in Jasper, then complete the journey to Vancouver aboard a tourist train called *The Rocky Mountaineer.* The *Mountaineer* only travels during the day. Passengers disembark at night to stay in hotels, then resume the trip the next day, when it's light and they can see the scenery.

I sleep soundly on this night, but awake to flashes of lightning. Rain pelts the window. Mindy, as usual, is already up.

"How did you sleep?" she asks.

"Much better. The motion of the train really didn't bother me" I reply.

"Yeah," she says, "that's because we weren't moving."

"Are you telling me we stopped most of the night?"

Mindy nods affirmatively.

I look out the window and remind myself to get into the Zen Train Mind state of oneness with the view. I see forest, then a river and a lake. When the train slows into another siding, I force myself to continue concentrating on the scene, jettisoning judgement. A dragonfly with iridescent wings paces the train, then easily darts ahead. I turn my attention to the geology. The land is much rockier here, with more relief. The forest is greener, healthier looking. The rock outcrops are a reminder that we are traveling over the Canadian Shield, some of the world's oldest rock formations. The shield is part of the continental crust. It is mostly buried, but here in Ontario the billion-year-old metamorphic and igneous rock is exposed. A billion years ago a massive mountain range with peaks exceeding 30,000 feet stood here, but erosion has left only the hills and a few exposed outcrops.

Meanwhile, the train's overall progress (at the moment not much faster than the erosion that wore down those six-mile-high mountains) is whittling away prospects of us being remotely on time. When I went to bed last night, the train had slipped to two and a half hours behind schedule. Now I can't be sure where we are because our progress is still through a largely trackless wilderness. Without a landmark, I can't get my bearings. I hope that Kristin's optimism of yesterday is true and that we are back on schedule.

We adjourn to the dining car and feast on a breakfast of blueberry pancakes. Outside, signs of civilization pass. We slow to a stop in front of the station for the town of Sioux Lookout. This can't be true, I tell myself, again realizing that this is not appropriate Zen Train Mind thought. I should be la-di-dah, but instead I can feel agitation rising in me like a Bay of Fundy tidal bore. We should have been at Sioux Lookout at about midnight; it's now 7:00 a.m. We lost another five hours during the night. Is that possible? No wonder I slept so well. Mindy was right about last night; the train barely moved.

But I remain in Zen Train Mind mode. I am sticking to it and not letting this schedule slippage bother me. Instead, I am thinking about our coming four-hour stop in Winnipeg. Nelly, a beloved second cousin of mine, lives there with her husband Juan and their six-year-old daughter Paula. Originally from Mexico, the Blancas found their way to Winnipeg in 2016 when Nelly was accepted to graduate school at the University of Winnipeg. She was almost finished with the program, and already had landed a job after graduation with Manitoba Hydro. They had now managed to survive their first Canadian winter and were eager for friends and family to visit them in their new home. Nelly had visited me years ago in Seattle, and I was eager to see her again and to meet Juan and Paula for the first time. I remember Nelly as being incredibly smart and wise beyond her years. It was not a surprise to hear that they were thriving in Canada. Juan already had secured a job as a woodworker and Paula was in elementary school. All were proficient, if not nearly fluent, in English.

# CHAPTER 11

## Big News: The Train is Late

THE TRAIN'S SLOTH is the worst-kept secret aboard *The Canadian*. From the beginning, the conductor has been a man of silence. The intercom remains strangely silent about our pace, only crackling to life when Claire checks in with some trivia about a landmark. Kristin seems to be avoiding me during one of my frequent forays into the corridor. When I do encounter her, she sticks to the company line that we will make up time. Maybe I can crack Claire, whom I spot heading to the lounge. No, she doesn't know anything about the schedule, but she's positively bubbling over about the wine tasting in the dome car after lunch. Don't miss it! Has the train slipped into an alternative universe? Has *The Canadian,* crew included, transformed into Zen Train Mind zombies? Am I the only one left behind, worried about the damn schedule?

The train slips out of Sioux Lookout at about the time it was supposed to ease into Winnipeg, still 250 miles to the west. I've kept Nelly informed about our lack of progress via my smartphone (cell coverage becomes more consistent at Sioux Lookout). The train's lack of progress also appears to be secret on VIA's website. According to Nelly, it is still listed as being on time. She discovered this the hard way by driving to the station in the morning when we were expected to arrive, only to learn that she would be lucky to see us by midafternoon.

Kristin wanders by as we finish our breakfast. Mindy, in her Mindy way, gives her a hearty good morning. But there is something wrong. Kristin doesn't have her usual buoyancy. She and other crew members have been working nonstop. Now it appears their shifts may get even longer; that is, if they will ever admit that the train is late.

"I have terrible news," Kristin says, solemnly. Mindy and I look at each other, our temporary haven aboard the train about to be interrupted by the announcement of some calamitous event. What could the bad news possibly be? Has the train hit another skunk? Is the world's longest freight train queued up ahead, waiting for us to pull over for the next five hours? Has North Korea attacked?

Kristin looks at us, dazed, and simply asks if we want juice with our breakfast.

"But what's the terrible news?" I ask.

"We are very late," she says. "We will have to serve lunch."

After Kristin wanders away, I turn to Mindy.

"That's the terrible news?" I say, relieved. "Like it's a big secret we are late."

Then again, it was Kristin who had been brimming with confidence that the train would make up the time, it always had in the past.

Mindy, always a little more sensitive to the plight of others, sees it in a different light. "I think they were all hoping to get to Winnipeg in the morning and chill out. Now they need to work an extra shift. Look how exhausted they all are."

She is right. I remind myself to slip Kristin a tip when we arrive in Winnipeg. That is the end of the line for her. We wouldn't see her again.

Our breakfast companions seem unfazed by the lack of progress. Larry and Elizabeth of Boston tell us that they had met a few years ago in a bereavement group. Both had recently lost spouses. Larry, an avid amateur pilot, learned that Elizabeth wanted to learn to fly. It was a match made, if not in heaven, at least in the sky. They also discovered they really liked Grand Circle Tours. They had been on more than a dozen. Every anniversary they go on a tour. This one has them aboard *The Canadian*.

The day passes with me checking the mileposts and comparing them with the timetable. I know I am completely off the Zen Train Mind, but someone must worry about this. I promise to do better after Winnipeg. Even the seemingly boundless patience of my wife begins to fray.

"Why do the freight trains have the right-of-way?" she suddenly asks.

"Because moving freight is important to the economy," I reply, instinctively taking the other side of the argument instead of joining my wife and castigating the freight rail barons. That explanation isn't going to wash with her. She continues, "But tourism is important, too. Maybe more important. They have such a national treasure in this train. They should improve on it. People should have priority over freight."

I can't argue with that, but the train gods can. Apparently, they are not pleased with the dissent emanating from the malcontents in Compartment F who want to mess with Canada's booming economy. As if on cue, *The Canadian* eases into a siding to wait for another freight train to pass. Our only solace is that we spot a pair of magnificent white swans swimming on a lake, increasing our bird count by two. Shortly after we cross into Manitoba, Nelly sends me a message telling me that the train is now allegedly arriving at 3:00 p.m.

# CHAPTER 12

## A Goose, a Rabbit and a Groundhog Wander into a Bar

THE CONIFERS THIN OUT as we approach the Great Plains. At the tiny farm town of Elma, the topography and landscape abruptly change: The train parallels Highway 15; the land smoothes out; forests are replaced by cultivated fields interspersed with groves of birch, maple, elm and poplar.

I study the plowed fields and contemplate a horizon that seems limitless, trying hard to return to Zen Train Mind after our brief insurrection about freight versus people. With laser-like focus, I stare out the window and notice a strange animal in a freshly tilled field. It's a brown, low-to-the-ground creature the size of a marmot, a groundhog or an armadillo. Nearby, I see a goose and a rabbit. It's a strange juxtaposition of creatures. The animals seem to be having a meeting. I point out this unusual trio out to Mindy, who is reading.

"Look at that," I say, pointing to the animals quickly passing from our view. "I don't know what the brown thing is. Maybe it's a groundhog or an armadillo."

"It is a goose," she says definitively, after a quick glance.

"No, it isn't. It is low to the ground. There is a goose nearby, though, and a rabbit."

"I definitely think it is a goose," says my wife, not looking up from her book.

By now the animal trio is out of view.

"There was a goose and a rabbit nearby. Maybe they are friends," I suggest, trying to be reasonable. "But there was definitely a third animal."

My latest statement leads me to wonder if there is a joke that begins: "A goose, a rabbit and a groundhog go into a bar . . ."

Mindy, seeing the beginning of my frustration, offers a compromise.

"Maybe it was a badger."

I think for an instant this might be plausible. But why would a badger, a species known for its ferocity and general lack of friendliness, be hanging out with a goose and a rabbit, both easy prey? Yeah, I know this is Canada where everybody, even animals, is extremely polite. Impossible, I tell myself. Besides, badgers live in the wild areas of Wisconsin where Mindy used to live. This alone is reason to suspect this as a possibility. Maybe badgers really don't live in Wisconsin anymore, but the notion sticks because the University of Wisconsin has adopted the badger as its mascot, which leads those who know little about the state to believe that badgers are a common sight when no one has likely seen a real badger in Wisconsin since the Civil War. No, I will not cave to the badger theory, not when the

University of California at Irvine has adopted the Anteater as its mascot. I know for sure there are no anteaters in Southern California, though sometimes I think the residents wish there were.

And this is how our conversation goes, morphing into the Theater of the Absurd. I wonder if I have taken the Zen Train Mind a station too far, overanalyzing what I observe. Thinking, at least too much, is probably not a good thing to do here, but then again, I am a novice. But one provocative thought does burst into my brain. I wonder if this is what marriage is all about? You see a groundhog. Your wife sees a goose. You concede a goose was present; yes, or maybe it was big white duck. Can there be compromise?

"Maybe it was an Australian sheepdog," Mindy says.

Outside, the train passes a field grazed by cows. No argument there.

"It definitely wasn't an Australian sheep dog," I counter, exasperation in my voice. "There were no sheep. It was a plowed field."

"How do you know that?" counters my wife. "Maybe there were sheep in the field, and the dog rounded them up, getting some exercise with his mates; the goose and the rabbit."

"Why would a sheepdog want to get extra exercise?" I say, trying desperately to convey logic to an illogical argument. "If I was a sheepdog and there were no sheep, I would take a nap."

"Figures," she replies.

"Okay, maybe it was a badger, or an anteater."

This conversation manages to pass some time as we rumble closer to Winnipeg.

The final approach to Winnipeg is agonizingly slow. The train gods are seemingly still angry with the communists in Compartment F and their "give the peoples' train the right-of-way" manifesto. We grind to the edge of the outskirts but then stop for 45 minutes in a freight yard. It is 3:00 p.m. I text Nelly and tell her we're near. Otherwise, there is nothing to do but stare at the undulating tall grass and attempt to decipher the various markings on the boxcars parked on the adjacent track, a good Zen Train Mind exercise. At last we move. Slowly, the backyards of suburban Winnipeg come into view: a man mows his lawn; a woman hangs laundry while a toddler rides a tricycle. A school lets out; yellow buses wait in the adjacent street as a stream of children pours from the building.

At 4:30 p.m., *The Canadian* finally eases into the Winnipeg Station. But we can't get off, not yet. Like anxious school kids awaiting a long-promised recess, we are lined up at the door vestibule ready to escape. But Kristin, who must keep the mob at bay, explains that she can't open the door because "the train is still on a live track." *The Canadian* is so long that it needs to be broken in two to fit into the station; until that happens, no one can get off. While the train shunts forward, then reverses, the conductor breaks his radio silence and tells us that our visit has been reduced from four hours to 45 minutes. *The*

*Canadian* will resupply and change crews as quickly as possible in hopes of making up lost time.

We pour off, welcoming the freedom to move our limbs on ground that does not sway unpredictably. Nelly, Juan and Paula, all smiles and virtuous in their patience, greet us at the top of the escalator that disgorges its passengers into the station.

## CHAPTER 13

### The Big Soda Can

THE TRAIN DOES NOT LEAVE WINNIPEG UNTIL 7:30 P.M., though prior to that there is plenty of back and forth—presumably to hitch up the part of the train that was detached during our arrival. I really don't know. I am happy to be in the dining car ready for dinner, with a fresh crew that appears to be all business. These people are ready to go. They want to gain back time as much as I do. Wait a minute! I'm not supposed to worry about these things. I took the vow. I'm aboard the Zen Train Mind!

The woman supervising the dining car is an improvisational genius. No longer do I have to guess which microbrews are on board. She has corrected the menu oversight by hand-printing the names of all the microbrews on a big piece of cardboard, which she hands to me. What it lacks in style, it makes up for in accuracy. I need my evening beer, but Mindy is more in the mood to sample one of the wines that are offered from Ontario or British Columbia. I have cash to pay for the booze, which is reasonably priced, but Tom and Carol, our dinner companions, ask to use a credit card. After an awkward silence from the server, she explains that the train is not yet equipped with the portable digital credit card machines common in every restaurant in Canada. Instead, she pulls out an ancient mechanical swiper gizmo commonly used in the last century. The machine makes an imprint of the raised relief credit card numbers. Except there is a problem: Tom has a new card; the numbers are not in relief. So much for conserving cash.

West of Winnipeg, the Great Plains start in earnest. Wizened spruce and bogs are replaced by freshly plowed fields. At Portage la Prairie, 50 miles from Winnipeg, we see an enormous replica of a Coke can, painted brilliant red, sprouting from the city center. Its ethereal shine reflects the last rays of sunshine. If the army sold advertising on its missile silos, this is how it would look.

Portage la Prairie owes its origins not to the Coca-Cola Company, but to the fertile soil and the railroad. The Great Plains, which spreads in all directions, was the habitat of millions of buffalo, antelope, deer and other wildlife when it was known as Rupert's Land and controlled by the Hudson's Bay Company. The Company discouraged settlement, believing that settlers would destroy the rich ecosystem that allowed the Indians to trap, thus providing it with a seemingly never-ending supply of beaver pelts. That changed in 1869, when, under the terms of the Deed of Separation, the fledgling government of Canada bought out the company's charter and began adding what would become the western provinces to the Dominion.[6]

Portage la Prairie sits on some of the richest agricultural soil in the world. Once the company relinquished its control of the west, settlers homesteaded the land. By the 1880s, thanks to the westward construction of the Canadian Pacific Railroad and the fertile soil, Portage la Prairie sported a population of 3,000.

The train's speed accelerates after leaving Portage la Prairie, adding some credibility to my speculation that this train crew means business. A double track appears, so there will be no stops for freight trains. We are running mostly due west, with a slight northward bias to angle us toward Edmonton. The sun sets, reflecting crimson off distant clouds. Gradually, the sky transforms from dark blue to gray. The morning's storm is long gone.

Despite the ongoing schedule slippage, which I officially no longer care about thanks to my heightened vigilance about imposing Zen Train Mind control, the new day begins on, if not a good note, certainly a reverential one. I emerge from my bunk to observe the plains of western Saskatchewan dotted with farms. We cross the Battle River and follow a valley bordered with rolling hills, flecked with trees and carpeted with grass. Oil derricks appear, hinting that we are near oil shale–rich Alberta.

Our breakfast companions are John and Ruth from Philadelphia. Like us, they enjoy train travel. Unlike us,

---

6  Alberta and Saskatchewan, previously part of the Northwest Territories, became provinces in 1905. British Columbia became a province in 1871.

they did not cheat by flying part of the way. Once they get to Vancouver, they plan to take a short Amtrak ride to Seattle, then board the *Empire Builder*, which will take them back across the northern tier of the United States. Another Amtrak connection will allow them to complete the last link back to Philadelphia, completing a grand circle around North America by train.

Shortly before breakfast arrives, John reaches across the table as if to shake my hand. We had already shaken when we had introduced ourselves, so I am surprised he wants to shake again. What the heck, I think, he's sure a friendly fellow. Besides, I am impressed with the way this guy plans train trips. Ruth extends her hand to Mindy.

"Let us pray," says John. Before I know it, I am giving thanks to Jesus for my breakfast. I normally am not a prayer type of guy, at least in the traditional way. And Jesus really isn't my man. But I decide I have nothing to lose, so I add a silent addendum to John's prayer. "Hello God. If you got any pull with the Canadian freight trains, please let us make up a few hours tomorrow. That's all I ask. Since you honored Moses' request to part the Red Sea, surely you could part a few freight trains to let us pass in the night. Amen."

# CHAPTER 14

### Adventure in the Shower

AFTER BREAKFAST, I am in the mood for adventure. Time for another shower. I want to bathe while Train Number One is hurtling west at 80 miles per hour, jostling over a track bed slightly warped from freezing winters and hot summers. This will be fun. My last shower was two days ago. Both of us timed our previous showers when the train was on a siding awaiting the inevitable freight train. It's time for a challenge.

Each sleeper car has a shower room, which (for us) is conveniently located next to our compartment. VIA provides each sleeper car passenger with kit bag containing a bath towel, washcloth, soap and shampoo. Unfortunately, the washcloths are missing from both our laundry bags, which were collected for washing in Winnipeg but not replaced. I press one of the attendant buttons but grow tired of waiting, so I bring my hand towel as a substitute.

The shower room is empty. I disrobe in the small dressing area, hang my clothes on the wall hooks, then step into the shower chamber. There is one faucet knob. I turn it to hot, then push it in. Nothing happens. I wait, while getting bounced around the chamber by the train's unpredictable lurches. I peer up to the nozzle and that's when a burst of cold water shoots into my face. I bounce off the fiberglass walls like a pinball, screaming profanities, a very un-Zen Train Mind-like thing to do. I am definitely not one with the universe, though I am clearly in the moment. It is unlikely that anyone has heard my shrieks, or if they have they most likely think it's the train whistle. After long agonizing seconds, the hot water flows through the pipes. I quickly finish my shower and exit.

"How was the shower?" asks Mindy, who has been joined by Andrea, our new attendant who answered my button call while I was being tortured in the shower.

"Refreshing," I respond curtly.

Andrea, like Kristin, is young, has an athletic build and oozes with the VIA cheerfulness. It appears no amount of lateness can faze her. She does tell us that the train's washcloth supply is exhausted. No worries, just use the hand towel, she tells us. I don't have the heart to tell her about the hot water delay in the shower. I don't want to do anything to discourage the crew's cheerfulness or cause a negative vibe that will slow our current warp speed. The plains of Saskatchewan are flying by, and with it comes hope that we will make up some time.

But Andrea does have one gripe. She reports that few, if any, of the passengers traveling with the two tour groups had bothered to ring the attendant to put their beds up for the day. In a sleeping car, this is standard train etiquette.

In the morning, before you go to breakfast you ring the attendant, and like magic, your room is ready for daytime use when you return. On *The Canadian* that means the bunks are stowed and the movable chairs are set up. The situation reverses itself in the evening when you go to dinner and return ready for bed. It's one of the many small pleasures of train travel and makes us appreciate an attentive steward.

"None of the tour passengers seem to know what to do," Andrea tells Mindy. "Now, we need to spend the afternoon getting all those cabins ready for new passengers in Jasper. Fortunately, I don't think we're going to get to Jasper until around midnight."

The original schedule called for a 2:00 p.m. arrival.

But what do I care?

## CHAPTER 15

### Zen Train Mind Derails, Again

WE STOP IN IRMA, ALBERTA, another town originally spawned by the railroad. Our freight train-less streak ends. I lock into Zen Train Mind, determined to get back on the wagon after the debacle approaching Winnipeg. I am doing well. Right now I have a nice view of a stagnant pool of water with giant cattails poking out. Across from the pond is a highway, and across from that is the forlorn Irma Hotel, part of its sign ripped away. The Irma Hotel is not a place I aspire to spend a night, so for the moment I am content in my box aboard *The Canadian.* Next door to the hotel is a house for rent, followed by a C-Store (The "C" presumably short for "convenience") and a restaurant called Dinner. Creativity in names is not an Irma strong point, though I am sure Irma has much more to offer. What can one surmise from a glimpse from the train window?

Enough, apparently, to slightly disrupt the space-time continuum of Zen Train Mind. My glimpse of the Irma Hotel at least provides me with an important data point, and data points are bad for me. I can't help myself. One data point leads to another, and before long my mind is wandering out of emptiness into a kind of spreadsheet hell. I calculate we are about 100 miles east of Edmonton, which means we are now at least eight hours behind schedule. My initial optimism that we made up time during the night as I slept with visions of double track clacking through my mind was wiped out when we awoke in Saskatoon at 5:40 a.m., and I realized we had not made up any time. On the other hand, we had not lost any more time.

A conversation with one of our dinner mates a few nights ago now seems more relevant than ever. John had told us that VIA warned him not to book on-going trips the day *The Canadian* arrived in Vancouver.

"But the train is scheduled to arrive at 9:42 in the morning," I said. "Surely you would be safe booking something that evening."

"The reservation clerk was pretty clear," John said. "She said the train's arrival was unpredictable."

"I booked a 5:30 p.m. Amtrak train to Seattle the day we arrived. I was wondering what we would do with all that spare time to fritter around with in Vancouver. I figured an eight-hour buffer was an eternity."

"Good luck with that," said John.

Until now, in Irma, I had thought we could make up that time or at least arrive in time to make the mad dash to the Amtrak train.

As the train pulls out of Irma, where we have spent at least 30 minutes, the loudspeaker crackles to life. Claire announces that we are in Irma, population 540, with farming as its main industry. Mindy's eyes flash; she has had too much Claire.

"Why is she always telling us stuff about the towns after we've left?!" says my clearly irritated wife. "And besides, most of this information is in the brochure. Let's hear something original for once!"

"Okay, calm down," I say. "It's been a long trip for everyone, even for Claire. It's probably not easy being an activity director on a train that is a kilometer long and eight hours late."

---

Seventy miles later we come to Tofield, identifiable from the sign of the town's funeral home and the IGA store next to it. Mindy points out wild pink roses growing next to the track. These become more discernible as the train slows, then stops. The intercom awakes after another long slumber, but instead of the activity director waxing poetic about the virtues of Tofield, the conductor's voice booms out. This is serious. We learn that our arrival in Edmonton, our next chance for exercise off the train, has been pushed back to 3:00 p.m. This makes us nine hours late. We also are informed that our scheduled 90-minute break in Edmonton has shriveled to 15, just enough time to add more observation cars to the train for the trip through the Rockies. This is interesting, because by my calculations Train Number One will cross the most scenic part of the Rockies at midnight. Why bother? Forget the extra observation cars. Shed the weight. Without those extra cars we can go faster; maybe we could even get our full 90 minutes of exercise time in Edmonton!

"Why are you so concerned with being on time?" says Mindy, not impressed with my proposals to get Train Number One back on schedule. "I thought you like to take the train because it's relaxing, and you can forget about things like being on time. You yourself told me time is suspended on a train, and now look at you. You're Mr. Nervous, clutching your timetable and calculating from your maps. Chill out! So, we're late; who cares? You're retired! What are you late for?"

In the deeper recesses of my brain I know she is right. But the shallow outer recesses are in control now. Animal instinct kicks in. I clutch the map and grab the timetable, thinking they might be snatched away at any second. These are the very instruments of my sanity and logic, the guardians of the gate that keeps the barbarian hordes away. I must know where I am!

Then some of Mindy's wisdom begins to percolate through that thick Canadian Shield-like cranium of mine. What does it really matter where we are or whether we are late? It's not like I have an important business meeting in Vancouver. So, we miss our Amtrak connection. There will be another the next day, and the day after that, et cetera. Contemplate what passes (we appear to be passing a rendering plant at the moment); see the struggling little towns with their little stores with fading facades and funeral parlors. Yes, this is what I must do if I am to shift my focus. I slowly fold the map of Alberta. Mindy peers at me as if reading my mind and sensing that a great transformation might occur right here in spacious compartment F.

The train, which had slowed to a crawl, now lunges forward like some giant animal jolted awake from a pleasant slumber. I snap out of my trance; my brain jolts back to its reptilian self. Just one last time, I tell myself. I will only obsess about this one last time, then I promise to be good for an eternity or until the end of time, whichever comes first. I tear open the map and greedily examine the timetable. I am like a drug addict who has been given his last dose of cocaine. I do the calculations mentally.

"I'm going to talk to the conductor," I declare. "He needs to know about my idea about ditching the extra observation cars."

"No, you're not," counters my wife.

She's right; I'm not. I sit and stew. Our sprint across Saskatchewan apparently was to little advantage.

"This means we will not get to Jasper until 11:00 p.m.," I say, glumly. "We will be in bed then."

"I know I will, but you might still be up, knowing you," replies Mindy. I can tell she is disappointed in my retrenchment from "relaxed Bob" and now realizes she will continue to share the compartment with a railroad timetable lunatic.

I tell her that I now think there is no hope that we will get to Vancouver to catch our Amtrak train to Seattle. It seems wise to cancel that reservation and try to snag a hotel room so we're not wandering around Vancouver late at night with no place to stay.

My brain is now in overdrive. I am coming up with my best plan yet. Mindy will be impressed.

"Maybe when we get to Jasper at midnight I can dash into the station with my computer and try to send a message to someone, explaining that we are being held hostage in a train in the Rocky Mountains, fed prime rib and salmon, and that there is a critical shortage of washcloths. I bet Trump will send in the Army."

"You're going to do this in your pajamas," deadpans my wife.

"I haven't been wearing my pajamas. It's been too warm. I've just been wearing my undershorts."

"So you're going to run into the station like a football player, with your computer tucked under your arm, in your underwear; this will be interesting."

"No," I reply. "You don't get it. It will be a diversion, so you can get into the station."

"Yeah, right. Why do we need to get into the station?"

"I don't remember."

With that, Mindy returns to her book. I glance out the window as rural north Alberta, its feedlots, big barns and green fields slowly go by. Then the train stops again, gives a lurch, and resumes its journey. For some reason, this engineer is a lurcher. The prior engineer started the train on a gentle, barely perceptible roll.

## CHAPTER 16

### The Edmonton Sprint

IT'S AFTER 3:00 P.M. when Train Number One penetrates the outskirts of Edmonton. Strings of tank cars are parked on the adjacent tracks. Oil storage tanks border the tracks. Next come big grassy mounds with "No Trespassing" signs, followed by a tangle of high-voltage lines. We cross the Assiniboine River and enter a zone of apartments and new home construction. Then the scene changes abruptly; amid a thicket, next to the railroad right-of-way, is a homeless encampment—a rare sight in Canada, at least from our observations.

We roll into Canadian National's Walker Freight Yard. The freight train on the adjacent track is composed of dozens of UTLX oil tank cars, each proclaiming that their owners are "The Tank Car People." I think this would be an excellent name for a rock group, a chemical industry punk version of the Village People. Below "The Tank Car People" declaration is the warning that hammering on the side of the car will "contaminate the product." Next come tank cars carrying sodium hydroxide solution (otherwise known as lye), highly caustic chemicals used to make everything from soap to explosives. Fortunately, The Tank Car People have provided phone numbers, conveniently stenciled onto the side of the tank, to call in case there is a spill. Next come cars "not for flammable liquids." What could they contain? Milk? Beer? How does anyone keep track of any of this? After the long line of tank cars are hopper cars that appear to have sat in the railyard for decades; wheat, grass and flowers are sprouting from the platforms above their couplings. Another freight train passes. Our train stops, then goes backwards.

"Maybe that freight train has our slot," says Mindy.

"I don't know," I reply, now in my relaxed "devil may care" incarnation. "Maybe we're going back to Winnipeg to start the day over again; like a railroad version of the movie *Groundhog Day*. Maybe the Tank Car People don't want to let us in."

"They're just dinging with us. Goldstein, this doesn't look good; I think we are both going to need therapy when we get home."

We back across a large highway and back into open fields. A man and a boy wave to us from a garden. At last, we back into a small station.

The Edmonton Station is puny, a mere afterthought of a building that looks like it was constructed in a day from a do-it-yourself kit. How could the same railroad that produced the magnificent Union Station in Toronto come up with this abomination?

Laptop tucked under my arm like a football, I shuffle

my way down the corridor as the train slowly comes to a halt. The vestibule is crowded with other passengers holding laptops, tablets and smartphones. We all have the same idea; we have 15 minutes to dash off the train to contact the outside world. For me, I need to cancel our Amtrak booking from Vancouver to Seattle, then book a hotel. I have jettisoned the plan to do this in Jasper. At our current rate, we might never get there.

I quickly size up the competition. A balding middle-aged man with a beer gut, clutching the latest in Apple Computer technology, and a bunch of grandmothers, including one fearsome matron sporting a cane with a brass lion handle. I will avoid her. Here is my plan: Outrace them all to the station, set up, log in and snag precious bandwidth before the rest of the gaggle arrives. This will be my last mission as "Timetable Bob." After this, I am coasting in on the Zen Train Mind. Really, I am.

When Andrea opens the door, we rush out. My competitors quickly fall behind. Some get stuck in a jam up at the door after I squeeze out. But once outside, I am not sure I am heading in the right direction. Train Number One is nearly a kilometer long and given the back-up to the station I momentarily think I am fast walking in the wrong direction. But then I see the tiny station in the distance. I pick up the pace. As I am about to ease into the home stretch, I glance back and see a millennial, whom I did not see in the vestibule, hair flying in the Alberta wind, closing the gap quickly. She must be six feet tall, all legs, buds stuffed into her ears. She must be frantic after having been cut off from the wired world for so long. Now we're neck and neck with a quarter of a train length left. But my 62-year-old legs cannot keep up with this new generation. I pull up, glancing behind to see the rest of my generation or older are still far behind. Besides, with broadband, there should be enough bandwidth for everyone.

I plop my laptop on a counter and quickly type in the password to the station's internet connection. The little circle on the screen goes around and around. Meanwhile, the others have arrived, and they too are mesmerized by the little circle or its equivalent, like zombies staring at our stupid, unresponsive machines. I give up. I shut the laptop cover.

Glen, who with his wife Iona had shared a lunch table with us on the first full day of the trip, is sitting across from me on a bench observing this scene of mass frustration. This is his stop; he's seen this before. They are waiting for their ride home.

"I don't think anyone has ever actually connected to the Internet at the Edmonton Station," he tells me sympathetically.

"How come this station is so puny? Edmonton is a big city. You would think they would have a bigger train station with broadband for all," I say.

Glen tells me the old station was downtown at the base of the Canadian National Tower. But that was built when there was more train service, including daily service to

Calgary. Now, with only two to three passenger trains a week (from each direction), the need for a big fancy downtown station made no sense to VIA, which sold the building and built this one-roomer on the outskirts of town. It isn't even on the main train line, which is why Train Number One backed in. But getting the train into the station is apparently much easier than it is for passengers to get in or out of the station on public transportation. At the time of our visit, there was no local bus service, which meant no city buses and no access to Edmonton's new light rail system. A national bus service is rumored to be planning a shuttle system to get passengers into the city center, which is five and a half miles away. Trying to figure out whether that service exists involves solving a series of unfathomable riddles on the company website. Compared with the bustling stations in Toronto and Montreal, both of which connect with subways as well as commuter rail, the Edmonton station lingers in the era when intercity passenger rail was on its deathbed. Indeed, in western Canada it doesn't appear to be recovering.

"You should see things in the winter," says Glen. "There are people lugging their suitcases in the snow to get to the nearest bus stop."

I make a mental note not to visit Edmonton in the winter by train.

# CHAPTER 17

### Surrender

AFTER ABOUT TEN MINUTES, the computer refugees begin to trek back to the train. At least I got a two-kilometer walk in. Once back on board, our progress is slow—extremely slow. I would make more progress, I think, if I walked beside the train along the track. An hour later, the train grinds to a stop in the same freight yard we had backed into earlier. The sprouts on the hopper car vestibules have grown a bit bigger.

"We've probably gone about a mile since the station," I note.

"You think," adds my wife. "But what do you care? Remember, you took the vow."

She's right; I did take the vow. We're not talking about the marriage vow, but the "control freak while on board a train" vow.

Okay, I give up. I officially surrender to the schedule and accept that we will not make our connection in Vancouver. I point out that under terms of the agreement I do get to make one phone call. I take advantage of the cell phone signal and dial my friend Ellie in Seattle, who puts me in touch with a Vancouver hotel. I cancel the Amtrak reservation. Now, I don't care how late we are. Really, I don't. There is no earthly reason why I must be home at a certain date or time or year. I have no job to return to, only a lifetime of doing whatever I want to do. And if it's sitting on this VIA train, then that is what I will do. At least I am well fed.

My secret prayer for a morsel of *Untitled Sheep* is answered at dinner. Lamb shanks highlight the dinner menu. They are good, very good, particularly when washed down with a microbrew. Dessert is a chocolate torte. I am mollified. I am relaxed. I am not even experiencing withdrawal symptoms. The schedule and map remain in their holder.

Entering the foothills of the Rocky Mountains, Mindy spots a beaver making its way through the slime of a green pool of water. I see it, too, and for once we can agree that we saw the same creature. How fitting to see a beaver, an animal that once flourished in most of Canada until Hudson's Bay Company trappers nearly wiped out the entire population so Europe's elite could wear fashionable felt beaver hats. Beaver skins became so valuable that in Rupert's Land, the common currency was the Made Beaver or MB. One MB equaled a good-sized beaver pelt. Fortunately for the few beavers that managed to escape the slaughter, silk overtook the MB in popularity after the Hudson's Bay Company surrendered its charter. The big rodents began a slow comeback.

—

No travelogue on train travel would be complete without a mention of the onboard waste-disposal systems. I am not one to dwell on this topic, but the toilet on *The Canadian* is unusual for the vociferousness of its disposal method. Of course, we are grateful we have a bathroom in our compartment; it eliminates those irritating nocturnal visits to the toilet down the corridor. The double-decker sleeper cars featured on most Amtrak intercity trains have bathrooms in the bedrooms, but not in the cheaper roomettes. This means you need to negotiate your way to the facility at night and *remember* which compartment belongs to you. Yes, they are numbered, but neither memories nor eyes always function properly in the wee hours. It's the memory part that worries me; it's only a matter of time before I crawl into bed with a stranger.

Not all trains are alike. On the *Lake Shore Limited* from New York to Chicago, Mindy and I wondered what the large wooden box to the side of her seat contained. Much to our horror, we discovered it was the commode. This meant special operating procedures during toilet time, as one of us would quietly stand outside the compartment while important business was conducted inside. On *The Canadian*, no worries; the bathroom is a separate room. It is the suction that impresses me.

"Have you ever watched that thing flush?" I ask Mindy after one of my trips.

She gives me the "I am not going to answer that ridiculous question" look.

"I haven't," I continue, "but I wouldn't want to be sitting on it when the flush went off. It would suck you right into the septic system. Man, that thing is powerful. It sounds like a rocket blasting off."

⁓

At dinner, one of our tablemates tells us that Justin Trudeau, the new Canadian Prime Minister, favors further development of the intercity Canadian train system to encourage tourism. We, as you know, have already discussed this topic 20 freight trains ago, and we heartily agree that this is a good idea. And why not? The scenery is beautiful, the food is great, and you never know what you might see out the window. So what if your arrival time is shrouded in mystery? Treat it as a guessing game, or start a betting pool on the expected arrival day and time, winner takes all! The PM needs to know from visitors that this is a great way to see his country; unhurried and stress-free (that is, once you purge your inner demons . . .).

*The Honorable Justin Trudeau,*
*Prime Minister of Canada*

*First of all, allow me to congratulate you on your recent election as Prime Minister; no doubt your father would have been very proud. When I saw your youthful visage on the news the other night, I called* to my wife. "Come look Mindy, the new prime minster of Canada is 15 years old!" I do not mean this as disparagement, but as a compliment because the world needs energized and committed youth to extricate the world from the environmental, political and social mess my generation has left behind.

We recently had the pleasure of traveling the length of your great country aboard The Canadian, the last passenger train to offer this excursion. One of your countrymen, with whom we had the pleasure to dine, told me that you were interested in improving the inter-city Canadian train system, particularly as a means of promoting tourism. My wife and I had numerous conversations about this very topic as we waited on sidings for freight trains to pass. Needless to say, we were much behind schedule, not that I minded much. Really, I didn't.

Let me tell you that you are spot on in this regard. Rather than get involved in the messy fight of priority of freight versus people, I suggest a solution that might be a win for everyone. Why not double track the damn thing! Yes, I know it will be expensive, but it should have been done a hundred years ago when the original transcontinental line was built. They single-tracked it because they were cheap. You would have thought the British Columbian goldminers could have spared a few pounds of the rock they were gouging out of the mountains back then *to pay for another track. How short-sighted! Now you, Mr. Prime Minster, have a chance to remedy this, and thus go down as one of your country's greatest builders. Yes, I know we Americans can't brag too much about our own rail infrastructure, or any infrastructure (any description of ours is usually preceded by the adjective "crumbling"). Don't look to your big goofball neighbor to the south for policy advice. Trust your own instincts on this one, young man. I say, Make Canada Great Again!*

*Warm Regards,*
*R.M. Goldstein, Retired American Admirer of Yours*

~

Mindy asks the wine steward if they ever make up much time on the last day of the trip. She looks at my wife as if she had asked whether trains could fly before shaking her head no.

We pick up speed again, rushing like the wind toward the front range of the Rockies. It is nearly 10:00 p.m., but still light. Around a bend through a break in the thick, lush vegetation, I see the beginnings of mountains; nothing spectacular, more like hillocks in the distance under a darkening sky. The forest is denser, thicker and generally taller and healthier than what we saw in Ontario. Littering the right-of-way is the usual assortment of dilapidated telegraph poles, wires akimbo, some collapsed by fallen trees. Rotten creosoted railroad ties lie in the swampy moat beside the track. On dry ground next to the ballast are piles of rusted metal plates, rails, fasteners and buckets. I mention this to a fellow passenger. We think a small fortune can be made from the recyclable metal strewn along the transcontinental line.

As darkness closes in, I spot a giant factory behind a thin façade of trees lining the track. Flames flare from a tall smokestack, giving the impression that Vulcan himself has set up shop. Is it oil? Gas? Methane? Then it is gone, hidden by distance and night. There are no subtitles on a train trip, and Claire, our activity director of all useful, if not timely, information, appears to have retired for the night. As we head further west, maintaining speed for once, I am surprised at the ease with which we appear to be ascending the Canadian Rockies. This mountain range, after all, was a formidable barrier when surveyors first began mapping routes over it.

## CHAPTER 18

### The Last Transcontinental Trains

IN THE MID-NINETEENTH CENTURY, the trails through western Rupert's Land's jumble of jagged mountain peaks, and the fords across its rushing rivers, were known only to the Indians and a handful of intrepid explorers and trappers. But during the wheeling and dealing to create the Dominion of Canada, the colony of British Columbia demanded that its price for entering the new union was the construction of a cross-country rail line linking it with the rest of the country. The newly minted national government said yes in 1871. The agreement promised British Columbia an operating railroad in ten years.

Like most massive building projects, the schedule was a pipe dream. The Canadian Pacific Railroad (CPR) company had been slowly building a line west across the Great Plains. The Rocky Mountains presented formidable engineering obstacles that would guarantee long and expensive construction. A survey initially favored a crossing at Yellowhead Pass, near modern-day Jasper. The main selling point was its relatively low elevation (3,711 feet) and reasonable grade. Another survey traced a route further to the south, which snaked over two much higher passes, Kicking Horse Pass (5,322 feet) near present-day Banff, and 22 miles further west, Rodgers Pass (4,340-feet). Kicking Horse was a railroad engineer's nightmare. It required a 4.5-percent grade (roughly 1 in 22, which later became known as the Big Hill), more than double the grade CPR originally promised in its original plan to entice British Columbia into the Dominion.

In the end, the southerly route won out because the Canadian government believed that a railroad line closer to the United States would better secure its territorial claims over a border that had only recently been established. Chronically short on cash, the CPR relied heavily on government subsidies and land grants to blast, fill and bridge its way across the mountains and rivers. On the morning of November 7, 1885, four years behind schedule, the last spike was pounded into the earth at Craigellache, British Columbia. Canada had its transcontinental rail line. Ironically, the spike was iron, not gold, perhaps a reflection of the budget-busting effort. In what might have been the shortest speech ever for such a momentous event, CPR General Manager William Van Horne, a man not given to long speeches, said the following: "All I can say is that the work has been well done in every way."

Van Horne's words, though few, may not have been true. In their rush to complete the line, the builders took shortcuts that would require years of follow-up work to straighten curves, build snow sheds and reconstruct bridges. In 1909, the CPR completed the five-mile spiral tunnel that wound down Kicking Horse Pass and eliminated the infamous 4.5-percent Big Hill grade.

But the flaws in the original work did not stop the CPR from starting passenger service shortly after the last spike was set.

The initial transcontinental services were called the *Pacific Express* (westbound) and the *Atlantic Express* (eastbound). The trains featured marble bathrooms, Venetian glass and Turkish carpets. Perhaps the luxurious amenities provided a distraction from the train's sloth-like pace across the mountains. The average speed of the "express" was only 21 miles per hour because it would have been suicidal to drive the train faster on a roadbed that hugged mountain bends and crossed hastily constructed wooden trestles. Once the service got under way, the CPR realized that the scenery of towering glacial peaks and pristine lakes drew passengers as tourists. Schedules were adjusted so that passengers could view scenery through the Rockies and the Selkirk mountains during the day. Large, opulent hotels were built along its route.

Despite the historic feat of linking Canada by rail, the CPR, like most big railroad companies of that era, was not a beloved corporation. The CPR had a virtual monopoly on rail traffic in western Canada, something that did not sit well with a lot of Canadians. Rival railroads slowly inched their way west, most notably the Canadian Northern Railroad. But the CPR had nearly a two-decade head start on its transcontinental line.

The Canadian government wanted a railroad company that was less focused on profits and more aligned with the national interests of settling the western part of the country. But the onset of World War I doomed the financial viability of CPR's rivals. The Canadian Northern and Grand Trunk railroads, both with extensive networks in Eastern Canada, faced insolvency. Desperate to stay in business, the companies merged to form the nexus of the Canadian National (CN) Railroad Company, a government-funded railroad that, during the following decades, would grow like a weed by taking over other failing railroads.

Soon after its creation, the CN started construction of a second transcontinental route over the Rockies to compete with the CPR line. The engineers dusted off the original northern CPR route over Yellowhead Pass and adopted it as the CN's western route. Bypassing Calgary and Banff, the northern line arced up to Edmonton, then crossed over the mountains to Jasper, the route we were on now. Initially, when the line opened in 1914, the rails turned north to Prince George, then west to the port at Prince Rupert. Two years later, another line was constructed south from Jasper that followed the North Thompson River south before turning west at Kamloops and then running to Vancouver.

The completion of the CN lines to the Pacific signaled the start of the great Canadian transcontinental railroad rivalry.

During the 1920s and 1930s, the CN operated the *Confederation* between Vancouver and Toronto, and also ran the *Continental Limited* between Vancouver and Montreal. For cash-strapped immigrants heading west to settle the prairie provinces, the CN also operated one-way ticket bare-bones "colonist cars"—sleepers. The rival CPR boasted four different daily transcontinental passenger trains along its route. Its marquee train, *The Dominion*, catered to well-heeled passengers who wanted to see the Rockies, and who might spend time at the CPR-owned Banff Springs Hotel or the Chateau Lake Louise.

The end of this era began after World War II, then accelerated in the 1950s with the expansion of the national highway system and airline service. Of the CPR transcontinental trains, only *The Dominion* survived the war. To modernize and make the cross-country trip faster, the CPR bought all new stainless-steel carriages. Sixteen hours were trimmed off the schedule. *The Dominion* was rechristened *The Canadian*, the namesake and forefather of the train we were now aboard. On April 24, 1955, *The Canadian* made its inaugural journey. Ironically, on the same day the CN, not to be outdone, debuted its new transcontinental service, dubbed *The Super Continental*. It just wasn't as super as *The Canadian*, lacking the luster of the sleek stainless-steel equipment and dome cars of its competitor. It wasn't until 1964 that the CN finally purchased dome cars, which were hooked on in Edmonton for the scenic journey across the Rockies.

But this was too little, too late. Canada's long-distance passenger trains were rolling down the track to extinction.

Although both passenger lines enjoyed some success in the 1950s, ridership nosedived in the 1960s as Canadians took to cars and airplanes. By the 1970s, the CPR and CN wanted out of the money-losing passenger service. Statistics tell the story. Total passengers on all CPR lines declined from 9.5 million in 1954 to 5.3 million in 1970. The decline was similar in magnitude for the CN. Desperate to stem the losses, the CPR petitioned Ottawa to allow it to discontinue *The Canadian*, but the request was denied, even though both *The Canadian* and *The Super Continental* were losing millions of dollars a year, threatening to derail the lucrative freight hauling businesses of both railroads. Clearly, the situation could not continue. In 1978, the government finally relented. It created VIA Rail Canada, a government-subsidized business, which took over passenger train service from both railroads in much the same way Amtrak had done several years earlier in the United States.

*The Canadian* and *The Super Continental* continued to operate daily until 1990, with the former's eastern terminus being Toronto and the latter's being Montreal. Both lines continued to lose money, though now the losses were assumed by the government, which was under constant political pressure to cut service. In 1990, VIA discontinued *The Super Continental,* leaving *The Canadian* as Canada's last transcontinental train line.

Perhaps the most significant change from the passenger's perspective was the switch in routes. *The Canadian* moved to *The Super Continental's* northern route, which bypassed Banff, Calgary and Regina, and added stops at Edmonton and Saskatoon. This meant that passengers would no longer see the spectacular southern crossing over Kicking Horse and Rogers passes, nor would they experience the marvel of the five-mile spiral tunnel, one of the great railroad engineering feats of its time. Because the northern route was longer, the trip would take four nights instead of three.

While the northern route has its high points, I am partial to the south. I rode *The Super Continental* in the early 1980s. I still remember the blue ice of the glaciers, the snow-capped peaks and the long darkness of the spiral tunnel. It was a grand journey and I am sad that it is no longer with us, another in the growing list of disappearing passenger train lines.

⁓

At 2:30 a.m. I awake. The train stands still. Yellow glare from bug lights slants in from the half-closed curtain. In my bleary state, I crawl to the window to peek outside. I am reminded of a scene from the movie *Casablanca*, where the hero, Rick (Humphrey Bogart), desperately searches the platform at the Paris train station for Ilsa (Ingrid Bergman). In the movie, the station is a scene of frenzied and panic-stricken passengers lugging suitcases, desperately searching for their carriages in a last-ditch attempt to escape the invading Nazi army. Well, maybe that's a bit of an overstatement because there is no advancing enemy army. The motivation of scurrying passengers and crew on Jasper's platform is provided by the inconvenient truth that it will be another three days before another westbound train crawls into Jasper. These poor people have been waiting around for 12 hours for *The Canadian*. It's a little too much for a groggy mind to comprehend, so I shut the curtain and go back to sleep.

# CHAPTER 19

### The Thompson River Canyon by Day

THE NORTH THOMPSON RIVER RAGES OUTSIDE. The winter has been long and wet in the Pacific Northwest, and now, in the spring, the Thompson is thick with brown runoff and telephone pole–sized trees surfing through its rapids. This is not a river for a casual swim. Through gaps in the forest, I see snow-capped peaks. But views of the big granite spires of the Rockies are far behind us, a victim of our tardiness and night.

The dining car at breakfast is nearly empty. It appears more passengers departed at Jasper than embarked. We sit opposite Ben, a big friendly Australian, who is touring Canada. He's smitten with the country and plans to return. A heavy machine operator, most recently from the bustling open-pit mines of western Australia, Ben tells us he had a job interview at a gold mine at Kirkland Lake in Northeastern Ontario. He has a skill that is in demand, so his talent is easily transferred from continent to continent.

"Computers can't do everything. Some jobs, like maneuvering these big machines to do delicate tasks, still need a lot of human skill," he tells us. "Just before I left

Australia, I had a job where we had to dig around a gas main. You can't program the machine to do that fine of work. If you aren't a skilled operator and make a mistake, you'll blow up the city."

Like virtually all the other passengers we met, Ben prefers the slow, albeit erratic, pace of the train. After this trip he plans to visit first Whistler and then Victoria before the long flight home, which he isn't looking forward to.

"I'm a big guy, about six feet, two inches. I can't even get my feet under the seat in front of me in economy class. I have to sit with my feet splayed, with my hand wrapped around my chest, like a mummy," he complains.

He says he has heard of a lawsuit filed against one of the airline companies by a small passenger who was wedged into a middle seat between two large passengers on the marathon flight between Australia and the United States (14 to 16 hours of flight time). Apparently, he was wedged in so tightly that he injured his back. The suit, according to Ben, alleges the seats are too small to safely accommodate passengers.

"At least on the train you can move around and see the country," he says.

Ben asks us about Seattle. He wants to know if it is near the mountains (yes) and whether those mountains contain bears (yes). "I'm afraid of bears," he says. "We don't have big bears in Australia, only those cute little koalas. They spend most of their day sleeping in trees."

I assure Ben that the black bears of Washington state

are shy creatures. Given Ben's size, he could probably win a wrestling match with one.

"When I hike in the Cascades, the last thing I worry about is bears," I tell him. "But it seems there are more dangerous creatures in Australia. What about all those poisonous snakes?"

"Oh yeah, the snakes," says Ben dismissively. "If you just stomp your feet on the ground they slither away."

After breakfast, we head back to our compartment. Our path is momentarily blocked by Andrea, who is suspended above the aisle, her feet balanced on the opposite seat armrests like a gymnast ready to dismount with a backflip. She is making up the upper berths for the day's configuration.

"How did you sleep?" she asks, cheerful as ever.

"Not bad," I reply. Mindy nods as well. As we get used to the nuances of this train's night noises and motion, each night we sleep deeper and longer. The noise is not the problem, as the VIA-supplied earplugs are terrific. The problem is my 62-year-old bladder and the sonic-boom flush of the toilet.

"Good," she says. "We asked all the passengers getting on last night in Jasper to be quiet."

At the village of Birch Island, nestled in the Thompson River Valley, I momentarily break my Zen Train Mind trance. I can't help myself; just one last calculation! I must know! After all, we may be going for the record! Now I want to be as late as possible. We are 13 hours behind schedule, slowly edging into oblivion.

I am done with that business now. I check back into the zone of tranquility and observe the confluence of the North Thompson and Clearwater Rivers. The powerful combination forms a mighty torrent that laps at the trees perched on the bank and inundates sandbars. Cow parsley, salmonberry, foxgloves, buttercups and wild pink roses bloom in profusion along the right-of-way. The conifers here are huge compared to their undernourished cousins in Ontario. I see Western Red Cedar, evidence that we are approaching the Far West. Sometimes the forest parts to reveal farms with bright green pastures and grazing horses. In the distance is a snow-capped mountain. A sudden silvery flash blocks our pristine view, then we hear the whoosh as the eastbound Train Number Two passes. It appears to be on time (not that I'm keeping track of these things anymore; really, I'm not).

Because we were supposed to be at our destination by now, lunch is an improvisation, our selections few. I suspect the dining car chef is attempting to figure out how to stretch what's left in the larder. Our choices are a chicken burger and salmon salad. The menus have disappeared.

I quiz the crew about the record for being late. I suspect it is within our grasp. If only the damn train would slow down! Mindy gives me the fisheye. It's just for fun, I mouth at her. She doesn't know about the record. She doesn't know that it is within our grasp, just a few more freight trains and it can be ours!

Our dining car server, a young black woman, says this is only her second trip, so she doesn't have much of a track record. Another waiter with more experience chimes in that an 11:00 p.m. arrival is his personal worst. Andrea, who once again is helping in the dining car, tells me this might be the record-breaker. She says with a straight face that the train is usually on time. Sometimes it's early. Yeah, right.

I like Andrea and am particularly impressed by her feats of gymnastic agility on a moving train. Her good mood is almost infectious. But when it comes to her analyses of Train Number One's pace, she clearly has consumed too much of the corporate happy drink.

In the early afternoon, the North Thompson combines with the South Thompson to form a formidable torrent. The mountains are barren, desert-like hills, the conifers replaced by sage and salt brush. Our stop in Kamloops is once again reduced to the bare minimum, but it's enough to allow us to step off the train and stretch our legs. Mindy and I head toward the front, where a fuel tanker truck (are these The Tank Car People?) has pulled alongside the engine. A lone attendant in overalls unhooks the hose from the tanker, finds the gas cap to the engine and starts pumping diesel. This gives me a few minutes to compose yet another helpful letter to the VIA high command:

*Dear Yves Desjardin-Siciliano,*
*VIA President and Chief Executive Officer,*

*Me again, the American Pest. I just can't let this go. I have tried very hard to weather the waits on sidings, watching Canada's economic might pass us. I even have adopted a new philosophical outlook to life to cope with my particular desire to be on time. While the crew is reluctant to concede that the train might be late, the evidence strongly suggests otherwise. Your own website tells us that Train Number One only arrives on time 35.2 percent of the time, even taking into consideration the rather liberal definition of "on time" that VIA has adopted; that is, arrivals within 60 minutes of the scheduled time are considered on time. Given the current performance of Train Number One (which I am still aboard, by the way), I would gladly triple that tolerance and call it even. Okay, so the current data is from 2016, but given that you are six months late posting this year's data seems rather consistent with present reality. I am not the only one who has noticed this trend. I quote from the May 17 issue of The London Free Press: "If you travel across Canada using VIA Rail and arrive on time, consider yourself lucky—your odds of doing so are worse than winning some of Ontario's lotteries."*

*I know, I know, it's the freight priority that is doing you in! I have already made a brilliant proposal to your Prime Minister to address this problem. Given that it might take 20 years to blast another 10 feet of right-of-way through the Rockies and the Continental Shield, here's an idea that might help in the interim. If you're going to be late, let's turn the situation to our advantage. Let's put on a show! While The Tank Car People gas up the engine in Kamloops, why not have the fuel attendant dance a little soft shoe number around the engine, or maybe even a Michael Jackson moonwalk thing, a little shimmy and shake along the fuel line. Stage The Tank Car People Band on the roof of the helper engine, with the chorus and lead singer leaning out the doors of the baggage car. Maybe add a Bollywood thing with some of the nimbler passengers. I even envision Andrea, or another one of your Olympic-rated stewards, back-flipping along the top of the passenger cars. Plenty of time to rehearse with all those freight train pullovers. Come on VIA, let's think out of the box!*

*Respectfully Yours,*
*R.M. Goldstein, Retired*
*Your American Pest Friend*

*P.S.: I have the phone number of The Tank Car People somewhere around here, should you need it.*

The train has grown by four cars since we left Edmonton. It is now 26 cars long, not counting the two engines.[7] A panorama car has been added, as well as three new sleeper carriages. I'm not sure why the sleepers are needed, as it seems there are fewer passengers after Jasper. Maybe they will be needed in Vancouver for the return trip in a few days.

Resuming the journey, Train Number One continues to skirt the Thompson River. Mindy and I take positions in the dome car. We want to get a good view of the coming canyon country. It isn't long before our vantage point pays a dividend. I spot a herd of about a dozen bighorn sheep lounging on a rocky outcrop next to the track. The sheep seem unfazed by the slowly moving train. In fact, I can imagine the dominating topic of conversation among herd members. "It's late again!"

A few minutes later, Claire comes bounding up the stairs, to tell us we are in for a special treat.

I was hoping she would tell us that the chef got a good deal on prime rib in Kamloops and that would be our featured extra meal. What a great way to end an extra-long trip! But that is not the case.

"Because the train is so late, we normally go through the Thompson and Fraser River Canyons at night. But you're going to get to see them in the daylight," she exclaims.

"Yeah, but look what we missed," deadpans one of the

---

7   I was tired when I tried counting the cars on the train. Do you count baggage cars? How about helper engines? The train was so long I couldn't really see to the end, so I kind of guessed. Does it really matter? I know someone at VIA will somehow get ahold of one of the 26 copies of this book that will be published, read it clear through to this section and exclaim, "Train Number One never has 26 cars! What was this guy smoking in Kamloops?" Let's just say it was a really long train.

English passengers.

The sheep sightings become more numerous and are augmented by herds of mountain goats. The freight traffic is also growing. Two-mile-long freight trains snake along the CPR tracks on the other side of the river, while on our side we pull into a siding every 30 minutes to allow a long freight train to pass on our side.

Meanwhile, the canyon grows deeper. I am not a geologist, but the canyon walls here appear to be nothing more than compact clay and silt, interspersed with layers of cobbles and boulders. Water has carved steep fins and deep fissures. At some precarious points, engineers have designed sheds to shield passing trains from falling rocks. Looking up, I see rocks tumbling in small avalanches, puffs of dust marking their descent from the upper reaches of the canyon. Some of the puffs cascade all the way down, banging against the roof the train. The passage reminds me of the train ride once featured at Anaheim's Disneyland through a fake Southwestern landscape of rocks dangling from cliffs amid bands of wandering Indians and cowboys. Railroad historians note that the Canadian Pacific laid its tracks on the more suitable side of the Thompson. When Canadian National decided to build its transcontinental line some years later, it had to take the remaining, more precarious, right-of-way on the opposite bank.

Journeying through this area at night might not be a bad idea for the sake of the passengers, many of whom are suspiciously eyeing the precarious position of boulders and rocks high on the canyon walls, and dust clouds from small rock avalanches. The fear is not unjustified. In 1880, a massive rockslide formed a massive debris dam on the Thompson that created a temporary 14-kilometer-long lake. A marker alongside the tracks shows that the water level reached to the top of the train's carriages. The railroad has taken precautions to ward off or warn of rockslides. Besides the sheds and numerous tunnels, I see that many of the lower slopes are covered with immense wire screens to help stabilize the slope. There also are detection systems that alert oncoming trains of rocks on the track.

On the opposite side of the canyon, across the Thompson, which is now seething with brown rapids, I spot a sleek blue passenger train with an abundance of large-windowed observation cars traveling in the opposite direction. This is the *Rocky Mountaineer*, the high-priced tourist train that plies the old CPR route to Banff via Kamloops. The train does not travel at night, as passengers debark for hotels, then resume their journey in the morning. Some parts of the tour are traveled by bus. While I can argue eloquently for a ride on a "real" train, I give credit to the operators of the *Rocky Mountaineer*. At least they saw fit to run one of their luxury trains on the spectacular southern route through the spiral tunnel to Banff.

A few catcalls from the crew wafts up into the dome

car as the rival train disappears in a streak of blue and silver. Good to see that a healthy rivalry exists. We, after all, are aboard a real train, one that doesn't need to rest at night. We are train people, not bus people. Let's be clear about that. I take heart that Mindy and I are about to finish crossing Canada in a first-class sleeper, for less than half the price of the cheapest *Rocky Mountaineer* excursion, which only shuttles tourists around British Columbia and Western Alberta. *Rocky Mountaineer* passengers will never know the adventure of sleeping on a moving train at night or using a toilet that sounds like an Apollo rocket blasting off. So what if our train is 13 hours late (not that I have an opinion on the matter)? But hey, we're still moving forward. We're going to make it—eventually. Yes sir, watch us go![8]

---

8   I confess that when I got home, I couldn't resist reading the Rocky Mountaineer website. I admit they offer attractive trips. I think these would be in the luxury category, so I am not sure you will find me aboard anytime soon, but I will not hold it against you, dear reader, if you succumb.

# CHAPTER 20

## We Would Rather Take the Train

IN THE LATE AFTERNOON, we reach the confluence where the now dark green waters of the Thompson are subsumed by the massive muddy torrent of the Fraser River. The canyon walls, here solid granite, funnel the water into a churning mass tossing about more drowned tree trunks like matchsticks in a washing machine. The sage and sedum of the desert are now replaced by Ponderosa pine and grass in the upper reaches of the canyon.

In 1884, this stretch of canyon was the locale of one of the stranger tales to emerge from the building of the railroad. Although various versions of the story exist, here is the gist: A train crew found an injured ape-like creature lying on the tracks, or spotted the creature near the right-of-way, and gave chase. The creature was captured, then taken to the jail in the nearby town of Yale, according to an account published in the *Daily British Colonist*. The newspaper reported that Jacko (they gave it a name) was four feet, seven inches tall and weighed 127 pounds, and was "something of the gorilla-type." The article described a creature with glossy hair and possessing incredible strength. Hearing of the capture, curious townspeople gathered at the jail. They demanded to see the creature but were told it had escaped. Early in my newspaper reporter career, I interviewed Grover Krantz, a Washington State University anthropology professor and bigfoot enthusiast. Krantz told me he corresponded with the grandson of a man who claimed to have seen Jacko. The grandson verified the story that appeared in the newspaper. Whether Jacko was an escaped gorilla, a teenage Bigfoot, the figment of someone's imagination or a tall tale remains a mystery.

In the dome car, the situation is getting downright jolly. Most of us have been on the train together for the entire journey. We've shared meals and bumped into each other in the aisle numerous times. A sense of community has emerged, thanks to the proximity of the bar, which is downstairs. Ben, the Australian, is buying drinks for a couple of New Zealanders. The Germans and the Dutch are on their second round, while the English chap observes to Ben, "I thought there was a rivalry between the Aussies and the Kiwis." "I know, it's true," responds Ben, "but we're in Canada, so I think I can make an exception."

Our dinner call comes as we approach Hell's Gate, the Fraser's most famous rapid.

We sit across from Margaret and Loren. They are older than us, and at first appear to be rather dazed by the menu, which is brief and presented to us orally by the server. It appears the chef has cobbled together one last miracle, with the only provisions remaining on the train. I end up with a salmon arranged in a donut shape with a center filled with vegetables and nuts. Mindy has chicken kebabs with wild rice. Finished off by a chocolate torte, our second unscheduled meal is a success.

Our dinner companions, who hail from Edmonton, plan to visit grandchildren who live in Victoria. Loren is hoping that the Victoria-bound bus that is supposed to meet them at the Vancouver Station will still be there when they arrive. Holding at about 13 hours behind schedule, I think this a rather shaky bet. But I figure they have already made alternative arrangements, as have we. No need to dwell on the train's tardiness. Let's just enjoy the remainder of the journey, I think to myself, pleased that I remain aboard the Zen Train Mind.

"Are you planning to return to Edmonton by train?" I ask.

Loren looks at me as if I am crazy.

"Did you see all those rocks above the track after we left Kamloops?" he asks.

Loren apparently wasn't in Zen Train Mind mode when we passed through the Thompson River Canyon.

At the town of Hope, the Fraser River Canyon begins to broaden, opening into a green valley. The river, only a few hours ago a seething torrent, is now broad and peaceful. Log booms line the banks. Clouds hide the mountaintops.

Darkness descends as we enter the outskirts of Vancouver. As the train crosses the Fraser one last time, we catch a glimpse of the city's skyline a few miles away. The train, as seems to be its tradition, is creeping to its end. The intercom crackles to life one last time. Once again, the conductor explains that the train's length will not allow it to fit on the station's platform in one piece. He asks us to remain in our seats until shunting and decoupling is complete.

"What's another few minutes," I mutter, watching the station platform as it first appears, then slowly recedes.

The train finally comes to a stop. From our window, we can see that we are still in no man's land.

"Do you think we should leave?" asks Mindy.

"Well, they didn't announce they finished the shunting. He was pretty clear about waiting until that happened," I respond. "We might as well enjoy these last few minutes on the train." Mindy gives me one last eye roll. She is tired. It is time to end this trip.

We sit, awaiting the all-clear message from the voice above.

Several minutes pass. We hear Andrea bounding down the corridor.

"No one is leaving," I hear her say, a note of exasperation in her voice. "Hey everyone! You can get off the train now. We're here!"

We warily emerge from our compartments. It turns out we were not the only passengers waiting for the conductor's announcement. If Andrea had not come along, we would still be on the train. Realizing that we are free, free at last, we gather our bags and step off the Thompson Manor for the last time. Next, it's about a kilometer hike to the station. I note, for the record and only for the record, whatever that may be, that we arrived at 10:30 p.m., 12 ½ hours after the officially scheduled arrival time. Not that I am keeping track, of course. Hey, I'm retired! What's another day on the train? This Zen Train Mind stuff really works!

On the taxi ride to our hotel, the young Sikh cab driver is intensely interested in our journey. He wants to know the details of the engine's power. Is it a four-stroke or a two-stroke diesel? How much did the trip cost? When he hears that we've been on the train for four days, he gets quiet, as if quickly rerunning the numbers through his brain.

"And you say you came all the way from Toronto?" he asks, perplexed.

I can tell he wants to break the news to us gently.

"You know," he says, "you can fly, and it would only take four hours and would be a lot cheaper."

Mindy and I look at each other, visions of the Thompson River Canyon, bighorn sheep, the great Coke can and the solitary moose standing in the swampy wilderness of upper Ontario still lodged in the back recesses of our sleep-deprived brains. Sometimes, we just can't explain why we would rather take the train.

## Epilogue

WE ARE STILL MARRIED. I am still happily retired. My cancers are in remission.

We are still Train People, though we've had no more contact with The Tank Car People since the completion of our trip. We enjoyed our train trips across Canada so much that we plan to take another one, this time from Vancouver to Winnipeg. At Winnipeg we will take the train north, to Churchill, where we hope to see polar bears. Service between Gillam and Churchill was suspended in May 2017 after flooding damaged bridges and the railbed. Repairs began in September 2018. Service was resumed on October 31, 2018.

## About the Author

ROBERT M. GOLDSTEIN was born in Los Angeles, but grew up in Santa Clara, California, and it was there that his train adventures began—his first one being with a wooden toy train he was given by his grandmother. After graduating from Oregon State University in 1977 with a bachelor's degree in Technical Journalism, he worked as a newspaper reporter for the *Walla Walla Union Bulletin* and the Bellevue *Journal-American*. In the late 1980s, his career took a different direction after he earned his master's degree in Public Administration from the University of Washington. Since that time, he has held a variety of administrative posts in California and Washington. He retired as Chief Financial Officer of the Kitsap Regional Library System in 2017. He has traveled extensively and has published travel articles on Nepal, Bhutan, the Arctic and China. His critically acclaimed first book, *The Gentleman from Finland—Adventures on the Trans-Siberian Express*, earned Goldstein the Benjamin Franklin Award for best travel book published by an independent publisher in North America in 2005. His second book, *Riding with Reindeer—A Bicycle Odyssey through*

*Finland, Lapland, and Arctic Norway*, received the INDIE
Book Award Silver Medal. Goldstein and his wife, Melinda,
live in Seattle.